PENGUIN BOOKS

THE PERNOD GUIDE TO
LONG WEEKENDS IN FRANCE

Born in 1948, Andrew Sanger attended several schools, including the Lycée Français in London. After leaving school, he travelled widely and lived in several countries, especially France, where he still has a home. Andrew Sanger is the author of several guidebooks, including *Exploring Rural France* (1988), *South-West France* (1990) and *Languedoc & Roussillon* (1989), and is editor of two series of guidebooks. He contributes frequently to the travel pages of many newspapers and magazines, including the *Guardian*, the *Sunday Express* and the *Daily* and *Sunday Telegraph*, and is the editor of French Railways' travel magazine *Top Rail*.

GW00467450

THE PERNOD GUIDE TO
LONG WEEKENDS IN FRANCE

Andrew Sanger

PENGUIN BOOKS

PENGUIN BOOKS

Published by the Penguin Group
Penguin Books Ltd, 27 Wrights Lane, London W8 5TZ, England
Penguin Books USA Inc., 375 Hudson Street, New York, New York 10014, USA
Penguin Books Australia Ltd, Ringwood, Victoria, Australia
Penguin Books Canada Ltd, 10 Alcorn Avenue, Toronto, Ontario, Canada M4V 3B2
Penguin Books (NZ) Ltd, 182–190 Wairau Road, Auckland 10, New Zealand

Penguin Books Ltd, Registered Offices: Harmondsworth, Middlesex, England

First published 1992
1 3 5 7 9 10 8 6 4 2

Printed in England by Clays Ltd, St Ives plc

*This book is dedicated
to Gerry and Joshua*

CONTENTS

1. INTRODUCTION

A FEW days in France can make all the difference to life. This is especially true when summer holidays are either a fading memory or a distant prospect. The delights of France and French life are always there, in any season, and could hardly be easier to reach. Our nearest neighbour can be visited with little advance planning, and no sooner have you arrived than the exhilarating Gallic air of enjoyment, of quality, style and civilization begins to take its effect.

Even the smallest French towns are satisfying, with their relaxed bars and chic boutiques, their skilful *boulanger*, *pâtissier* and *charcutier*. At least one day a week – generally Saturday – there's the lively market to which farmers from the surrounding countryside bring a cornucopia of fresh ripe produce: fruit, herbs and vegetables piled high, cut flowers, traditional cheeses, free-range hens and eggs, farm-made potted meats and every other ingredient of the regional cuisine. In coastal towns, fish too, and vast quantities of crabs, oysters and mussels fresh from the sea, will be heaped on the market stalls. The chefs of nearby restaurants join with eagle-eyed housewives to see what's on offer and buy only the best. If you want to discover what can be done with all this good food, there is usually at least one first-class restaurant within a few minutes of the market-place, often with excellent three- or four-course menus at astonishingly low prices. In some towns there are dozens of such high-quality restaurants, while many a rustic village also has its good, reliable hotel-restaurant serving local specialities properly prepared.

Of course, there's much more to France than food and drink. Most towns, small or large, have made great efforts to preserve their heritage. Instead of our modern shopping malls and office blocks, French towns still have ancient central districts of narrow medieval lanes and shopping streets. It is sheer delight to

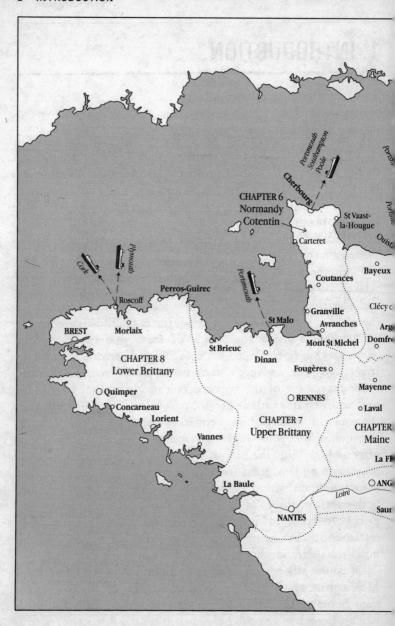

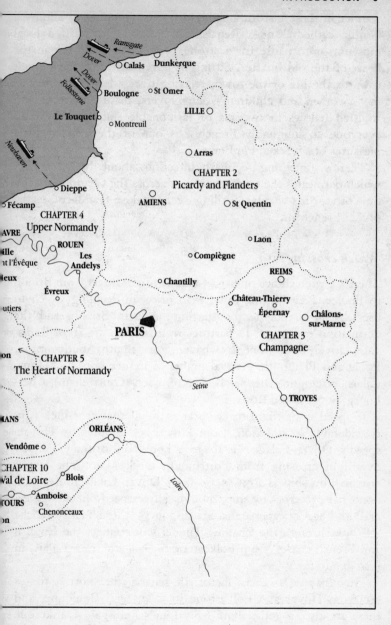

Ramsgate

Dover

Folkestone

Newhaven

Calais

Dunkerque

St Omer

Boulogne

LILLE

Le Touquet

Montreuil

Arras

CHAPTER 2
Picardy and Flanders

AMIENS

St Quentin

Dieppe

Fécamp

CHAPTER 4
Upper Normandy

Laon

AVRE

ROUEN

Les
Andelys

Compiègne

REIMS

Château-Thierry

ille
nt l'Évêque

eux

Évreux

Chantilly

Épernay

Châlons-
sur-Marne

utiers

PARIS

CHAPTER 3
Champagne

on

CHAPTER 5
The Heart of Normandy

Seine

TROYES

MANS

Vendôme

ORLÉANS

CHAPTER 10
Val de Loire

Blois

TOURS

Amboise

Chenonceaux

on

Loire

wander in these historic neighbourhoods, stopping to admire a
Gothic cathedral or a Renaissance mansion, to visit a local
museum or to pause for a strong coffee in a lively bar in the
heart of the old quarter. Sitting at pavement tables facing out
towards the life of the town, relaxing over a leisurely drink as
men, women and children, young lovers, mature matrons and
well-fed fellows in overalls or fashionable suits pass by (and
everyone so inimitably French!), is one of the greatest little
pleasures of a weekend in France.

There's something peculiarly infectious about the *joie de vivre*
which permeates the atmosphere just across the Channel. At any
time of year it's worth travelling over to take a few deep breaths
of that French air.

Which crossing?

There's a wide choice of cross-Channel routes direct from Britain
to France. Key factors, other than price, in deciding which to
use obviously include the starting point in Britain, and the
destination in France. Departures from Britain are from Ramsgate, Dover, Folkestone, Newhaven, Portsmouth, Southampton,
Poole and Plymouth. Arrival points in France are Dunkerque,
Calais, Boulogne, Dieppe, Le Havre, Caen (Ouistreham), Cherbourg, St Malo and Roscoff.

If speed is of the essence, bear in mind that crossings vary
considerably in duration, from a mere 35 minutes on Hoverspeed's Dover–Calais run to 10½ hours on Brittany Ferries'
overnight crossing from Portsmouth to St Malo. The fastest
crossing by ship is P&O's 1¼-hour Dover–Calais route. You
don't have to cross by ship, though. Hoverspeed operate hovercraft and SeaCat catamarans. Starting in 1993, the Trans-Manche
rail link through the Channel Tunnel will connect the English
and French coasts (from Folkestone to Sangatte, near Calais) in
just 30 minutes.

Price may be a crucial factor. In general, the shortest routes
are from Dover and Folkestone to Calais and Boulogne, and
these are also, together with Sally Line's Ramsgate–Dunkerque
route, the least expensive. Normal single or return cross-Channel

fares vary according to the length of the car, month, day of the week, time of day, number of passengers and age of child passengers. However, all Channel operators have lower prices for short excursions, and it is worth shopping around. Return tickets valid for three, four or five days are often a bargain. In addition, most Channel operators have a selection of Weekend Breaks with Channel crossing and half-board accommodation at an inclusive price. Check their current brochures.

At the beginning of each chapter, the most convenient Channel routes for that region are detailed.

Opening hours

In the north of France – everywhere covered by this book – most shops, offices and banks open at either 8 a.m. or 9 a.m. and close at noon. They reopen at 2 p.m. and close again at about 5 p.m. One of the variations from this pattern is that food shops often open earlier than 8 a.m.

Nearly all shops are open Tuesday to Saturday inclusive. Most are closed on Sunday (forget what you may have heard about the 'continental Sunday'!) and a great many are closed on Monday as well. The deviations here are that some food shops do open part of the day on Sundays, and pâtisseries in particular enjoy a brisk trade on Sunday mornings. *Hypermarchés* or *centres commerciaux* (hypermarkets) or big *supermarchés* (supermarkets) are generally open Monday to Saturday from 9 a.m. to 9 p.m. Most localities also have their fresh produce market on one or more days each week. Very often these take place in the morning only.

Museums and galleries for the most part keep normal office hours, but their usual weekly closing day is Tuesday. Many of them, in common with other tourist facilities and attractions, are open only from Pâques (Easter) to Toussaint (All Saints, 1 November).

What to buy

When shopping in France, look for style and originality, not just bargains. What the French do well, apart from the culinary treats, is dashing and delightful children's clothes, baby paraphernalia, quality kitchenware, equipment for wine enthusiasts, natty kitchen gadgets (the French love them), gorgeous lingerie (be prepared to spend £30 on a pair of knickers!), perfumes and attractive stationery. For anyone whose French is up to it, recipe books are good, and it's fun to buy children's books and cartoon strips to help children – and adults – learn the language. Cartoon strip books (*bandes dessinées* or *BD*) are very popular among all age groups in France and range from jolly Astérix stories to Bretecher's witty social comment to Wolinski's erotica.

While books, clothing and hardware may be bought at department stores, supermarkets and hypermarkets, the best of gastronomic delicacies are usually available only in specialist shops or *épiceries fines*. Among the food specialities worth taking home, look out for high-quality hand-made chocolates and other confectionery, traditional farm-made cheeses, preserved meats and charcuterie, and vegetables in jars for use in *crudités*. Pick up some ground coffee (better and cheaper in France than in Britain), olive oil, strings of garlic and ultra-cheap (but good) French beer. When buying wines, bear in mind that humbler varieties are the better bargain; the savings on more expensive *appellations* are relatively small.

Remember to discover and buy the gastronomic specialities of the region you are visiting: for example, in Normandy, farmhouse cider and Calvados.

Bon appétit!

The most enjoyable and most sensible way to eat in France is to walk into a clean, unpretentious restaurant already busy with French diners settling down at their tables and order a set meal. This is very easy and requires almost no knowledge of the French language. It is often said that, in choosing somewhere to eat, one should not be deceived by fine white table linen and gleaming silverware, and that many homely establishments can present an excellent meal. Although this is true, it has been my experience that the very best food is usually served at attractively laid tables.

Outside every French restaurant the *menus* and the *carte* are displayed. In France, a *menu* is a set meal with a fixed price. Most restaurants offer a choice of three *menus* at different prices (say, 60F, 80F, 110F). The price difference reflects not a difference in quality so much as quantity (that is, the number of courses) and ease of preparation. The *carte* is a list of dishes priced individually. It will include many things which are not on the day's *menus*. However, although eating *à la carte* (that is, from the *carte*) may give more choice, often it means that some or all of the meal will have emerged from the freezer, and that your bill will be much higher.

Local climate, soils and traditions have given every area its specialities. It's well worth ordering these. Ingredients come from nearby farms and these dishes capture much of the essence of the region. In addition, chefs are generally particularly adept at preparing local specialities.

The French take a rigidly conventional view of meals, which have a definite, unalterable structure. They begin with soup or hors d'oeuvre, and move on to cooked dishes (the first of which is the entrée); a simple green salad may follow, then comes cheese, and finally the dessert. Not all meals have all these courses, and it is quite usual to be offered either cheese or dessert, and not both. If fruit is served, it must come after the dessert.

Lunch is eaten from 12 noon to 2 p.m. (3 p.m. on Sundays), dinner from 7.30 p.m. to 9.30 p.m. Outside these hours, restaurants are closed and it can be difficult to find something to eat. The best bet for a meal at other times is a brasserie, where simple hot food is served all day.

A restaurant bill normally includes service and tax (the letters *TTC* mean *toutes taxes comprises*, all taxes included). Some menus state *Vin compris*, meaning that ordinary table wine is included in the price of the meal; this is usually a quarter-litre per person, often presented in a *pichet* (a pitcher or jug). Where a menu states *Boisson comprise*, it means that some drink other than wine may be ordered – usually beer, cider or a soft drink. Don't order coffee, tea or milk with your food (not even dessert), unless you want to be treated with scorn by waiters and other diners! After the meal is the time for coffee or *tisane* (herb tea). If you prefer, decaffeinated coffee (*un decaffeiné*) is available in almost every restaurant and bar.

For breakfast, elevenses or teatime, remember that it's quite in order in France to buy something tasty at a pâtisserie and take it to a café-bar (unless the bar sells cakes of its own). No one will object.

Santé!

In France, drink plays a vital part in life and is an essential lubricant for all social interaction. Yet it is rare indeed to see a Frenchman drunk; the French do not usually drink with the intention of getting drunk at all, but rather to enhance appetite, conversation and companionship.

There's nothing in France equivalent to either a 'café' or a 'pub'. Instead restaurants, brasseries and bars all serve the same drinks, and all are open to the whole family. In any bar, not just a multitude of alcoholic and soft drinks, but coffee, hot chocolate, tea and herb tea are equally available. First thing in the morning people on their way to work will stop at a bar for a *grande crème* (large white coffee) or an espresso. A few hardened individuals will knock back a black coffee with a dash of cognac or similar. The French keep themselves going by drinking coffee all day in powerful little doses. Tea is weak and of poor quality – no wonder they can't understand why the British like it so much!

Certain cooling thirst-quenchers are especially popular as the day goes on. For a bottle of one of the well-known German or Belgian lagers ask for *une bière*; a glass of draught lager is called *un demi* or *une pression*; a shandy (beer mixed with lemonade) is *un panaché*. You can always have *un verre de rouge*, a glass of cheap red wine. One of the most typical non-alcoholic drinks is sparkling mineral water – the most usual, in a bar, being *un Vichy* (in a restaurant, lightly sparkling Badoit and still Evian are the most common waters to accompany food). On request, the water may be brightly coloured with various sickly-sweet *sirops*. A *Vichy menthe* (mint), for example, is radiant green.

Syrups can be added to other drinks too, though purists will object. Even pastis (see below) may be served all sorts of curious shades.

Pastis is the inexpensive anise-flavoured spirit with which the French pass many a leisurely hour. A small amount is poured into the bottom of a tall narrow glass, which is topped up with water. Many people order pastis by brand name: Ricard is the best known; 51 is another leader. It's above all a drink of the warm South, and for northerners there's a touch of southern sun in the word 'pastis'. In the North it's more usual to ask for Pernod – which, however, is very much the same drink.

As mealtimes approach, comes the time for an aperitif. The usual aperitif hours are about 11.30 a.m. and 7 p.m. In the evening, particularly, this is a lingering moment of relaxation and talk. Pastis or Pernod, again, is one of the most popular orders. Other spirits are often taken at this time, notably cognac or whisky; the French are great admirers of a good Scotch. There are several brand-name aperitifs, for example Suze, Dubonnet and Martini, which are fortified wines fragrant with secret recipes of herbs and spices. A glass of white wine makes a cheap, simple aperitif; it can be cut with blackcurrant to make a *blanc cassis*. A *kir* is the high-class version, which should properly

be made (rarely is, though) with *cassis* liqueur from Dijon, and a
sharp Burgundy white called Aligoté. A *kir royale* uses champagne for its white wine. Of course, a glass of champagne on its
own is a tempting alternative, but pricey.

In the Champagne region itself, you'd be more likely to have
the local aperitif called ratafia, made from local grape juice laced
with *marc* (a powerful spirit, like *eau de vie*). Other areas also
have their local drinks – it's often worth asking for something
régional.

At the dining table, too, there is a strong local flavour. In
grape-growing areas, locally-made wines dominate. In much of
our Long Weekend part of France, wine is not made, and a
traditional alternative is on offer: cider in Brittany and Normandy, beer in Picardy and Flanders. In these regions, though
as elsewhere in France, most people nowadays prefer wine with
their food. The Valley of the Loire, Maine, the southern tip of
Brittany and Champagne all make their own wines. It's not
generally known that Champagne produces good-quality still
table wines as well as its renowned speciality.

After the meal comes the digestif, a fiery potion designed to
provide the finishing glow to a good meal. Various expensive
liqueurs may be chosen; but cognac, armagnac and Calvados are
all more usual, and are all essentially what the British call
brandy. Calvados, made from apples, is Normandy's local brew,
and on its home ground is sometimes served in the middle
of a big meal – a gastronomic intermission known as the *trou
Normand*.

Finding hotels and restaurants

A few especially tempting hotels and restaurants have been
recommended in the following chapters, but this personal selection merely hints at the vast range of excellent places available.

As well as the hundreds of palatial hotels offering luxury of
the highest order, there is an extraordinary abundance of good
low-priced hotels and restaurants in France, in both town and
countryside. In particular, there are tens of thousands of small
family-run establishments, while on the edge of larger towns

low-cost comfortable modern 'branded budget hotels' (as they are known in the trade) such as Campanile can be easily identified. All hotels are regularly inspected by local authorities and stars awarded, but the criteria are sometimes rather inscrutable, and many adequate hotels exist which fall well short of even a single star, while others far exceed the standard indicated by the maximum four stars. To discover which hotels and restaurants are worth using, it is helpful to consult a guidebook.

The red covers of the *Guide Michelin* enclose a compendious list of addresses from the cheapest to the most expensive, but all are recommended. All the information is given in symbols, explained in a multilingual key at the beginning of the book. Note when choosing a restaurant from the *Guide Michelin* that the knife-and-fork symbol reveals nothing about food but indicates a high standard of décor and service. For food which is far above the average standard, a rosette (or 'star') is awarded. Better places are awarded two rosettes, and the most outstanding food in France is indicated by three rosettes. The *Guide Gault Millau*, written in highly idiomatic and often rather scathing French, is the most highly reputed guide in France. It makes a selection of the very best places to eat and to stay, but has a penchant for things modern and creative, rather than traditional and dependable. The *Gault Millau* awards *toques* (chefs' hats) to exceptional restaurants, with up to four *toques* for the most outstanding places.

It can also be useful to consult the handbooks of the various French hotel and restaurant federations. The most important of these groups are:

Château Accueil (International Services, 8–10 Royal Arcade, London SW1Y 4UY, tel. 071-930 5551) – private châteaux which take paying guests.

France Accueil (10 Salisbury Hollow, Edington, Westbury BA13 4PF, tel. 0380-830125) – family-run hotels of reasonable standard in towns large and small.

Relais Routiers (354 Fulham Road, London SW10, tel. 071-352 5763) – recognizable by the distinctive blue-and-red circular sign outside, these are basic truck drivers' pull-ins offering good home cooking at low prices, and sometimes with a few basic rooms above the restaurant.

Relais et Châteaux (9 Avenue Marceau, Paris 75118, tel. 1.47.23.41.42) – classic old-fashioned luxury in magnificent hotels, and (especially those designated as 'Relais Gourmand') with excellent food.

Relais du Silence (2 Passage Duguesclin, Paris 75015, tel. 1.45.66.77.77) – high-quality hotels in quiet locations.

Logis et Auberges de France (83 Avenue d'Italie, Paris 75013, tel. 1.45.84.70.00, or through the French Government Tourist Office) – identified from outside by a distinctive sign representing an old brick hearth, this is the most useful of all French hotel groups for provincial towns and villages. It is a federation of some 5,000 family-run independent hotels, nearly all with a good inexpensive restaurant (half of them specialize in regional dishes); bedrooms are mostly of modest but comfortable two-star standard, and prices are reasonable.

Also well worth considering for more informal short-stay accommodation are **chambres d'hôte**. These offer bed and breakfast, often with evening meal too, in people's homes in country areas; they're no cheaper, though, than hotels of similar standard.

Hotels need to be booked only a few days ahead by a simple phone call, except in July and August and in popular holiday areas, in which cases it may be best to reserve a room several weeks ahead and confirm the booking in writing. Remember to specify if you would like *un grand lit* (a double bed) or *deux lits* (twin beds). Hotels almost always charge by the room, not per person. Prices must be displayed at reception and in the room itself (usually on the back of the door). Hotels expect reserved rooms to be claimed by about 7 p.m.; if you are likely to arrive after that time, telephone to let them know.

Two other interesting features of French hotels are that instead of pillows the bed may have a bolster (pillows, if any, and spare blankets are in the wardrobe), and that the usual hotel breakfast of *café au lait* and croissant or *tartine* (French bread and butter) will almost invariably be brought to your bedroom at no extra charge. When you are asked what you want for breakfast – 'Qu'est-ce que vous prenez?' – the question refers only to the hot drink you would like.

Driving and parking

The most crucial thing for British drivers to understand about driving in France, apart from driving on the right, is the principle of *priorité à droite*. It is extremely simple: you must give way to traffic coming from the right unless signs indicate to the contrary.

Four all-important signs relating to *priorité* are the 'yellow lozenge' (which shows that you are driving on a main road which has priority at all junctions); the yellow lozenge crossed through with a black line (this shows that the priority conferred by the lozenge is coming to an end); the triangle showing either diagrammatically or with the words 'Passage Protégé' that you have priority at the next junction; and the 'Give Way' triangle (with the words 'Stop', 'Cédez le Passage' or 'Vous N'Avez Pas La Priorité') showing that you do not.

A common misunderstanding among British visitors is the idea that the old French roundabout, at which traffic already within the roundabout gives way to vehicles entering the roundabout, has been scrapped. This is far from the case. At roundabouts as at all junctions, priority is still from the right unless there are 'Give Way' signs on the approaching roads. The current situation is that at the majority of roundabouts, except in city centres, there are 'Give Way' signs on the roads leading in. This situation is anomalous and potentially dangerous, since drivers already within the roundabout cannot be sure that they have the priority. The French are in any case very bad at roundabouts, many of which give no indication of where the different exits lead.

Priorité à droite is still much in evidence both on quiet rural back-roads and in town centres, where usually any vehicle approaching from your right, even a bicycle, has priority.

Parking regulations can be idiosyncratic: often it's permitted on one side of the road only, on alternate odd (*impair*) and even (*pair*) days of the month. Zone Bleue parking is allowed only on display of a *disque bleue* permit, for which you have to pay.

After (or better still, before) a good lunch or dinner bear in mind that there are swingeing on-the-spot fines for speeding and drunkenness, and you may be required to stop travelling until considered sober.

Speed limits are 130 kph (80 mph) on toll motorways, 110 kph (70 mph) on free motorways and dual carriageways, 90 kph (56 mph) on other roads except 50 kph (30 mph) in built-up areas. There's a *minimum* speed of 80 kph (50 mph) in the outside lane of motorways in normal weather conditions. French Government Tourist Offices abroad give out a leaflet, 'Motoring in France', detailing rules of the road.

Tourist information

The French Government Tourist Office at 178 Piccadilly, London w1v 0AL, has a huge quantity of free information on the French regions, general information about France, a useful quick reference guide for visitors, local maps, etc. Send 80p for post and packing when requesting brochures or information.

Almost every French town has its **Syndicat d'Initiative** or **Office de Tourisme**, which is a local information centre with helpful, knowledgeable staff.

2. PICARDY AND FLANDERS

Nord, Pas-de-Calais, Somme, Aisne and Oise

Getting there

A succession of ferries runs round the clock every day of the year (except Christmas Day) from Folkestone and Dover, with frequent crossings – up to about thirty a day – to Calais and Boulogne. Scheduled journey times by P&O or Sealink ferries range from 1¼ hours to about 1¾ hours; and because the trip is so short, delays caused by bad weather rarely amount to much. A third route from Ramsgate to Dunkerque, on Sally Line, takes 2½ hours. It arrives, not at Dunkerque itself, but at Gravelines, on the Dunkerque–Calais coast road.

Although not within the region, Dieppe should not be discounted as an arrival port for southern parts of Picardy. Dieppe is 4 hours from Newhaven on Sealink, with usually about four crossings daily (fewer in winter).

Two much faster alternatives to the ferry are operated by Hoverspeed. Both are more expensive than travelling by ship. One is the hovercraft, which on a fine day can cross from Dover to Calais or Boulogne in just 35 minutes, touching almost 70 mph; on a rough day, though, it's a bumpy ride, and travels at barely half the speed (which still compares well with a ship). The other is the SeaCat, largest catamaran in the world, which also plies from Dover/Folkestone to Calais and Boulogne in 35 minutes. The hovercraft run during daylight hours only; the SeaCat operates throughout the night as well. Yet another possibility (from 1993) is to put the car on the Trans-Manche Link and head through the Tunnel: you'll emerge at Sangatte, near Calais, half an hour later.

QUITE apart from its many other attractions, this corner of France has one clear advantage for a leisurely short break: it is quick and easy to get to. After all, the white cliffs of the Côte d'Opale are less than 20 miles from Kent. Thanks to this ease of access, no other part of France receives so many British visitors as the broad northern landscapes of Picardy and Flanders. Yet few regions remain so unknown. For most travellers, this is an area not to linger in but merely to cross, on the fast autoroutes which cling to the high ground under vast skies, revealing none of its secrets.

This region is perfect for a quick dip into French life. It's good at any time of year, too, including winter, because Picardy and Flanders are well versed in the pleasures of remaining

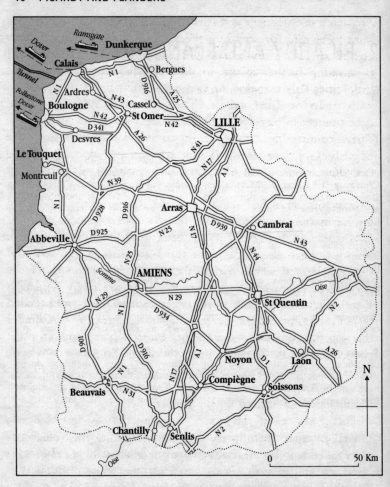

PICARDY AND FLANDERS

indoors. The main points of interest are restaurants, bars, museums and fine cathedrals. Out of doors, autumn and winter days can be still and crisp, and there are many beautiful beech and oak woods crossed by footpaths. A good walk, and a return to a warm hotel in time to get ready for an excellent dinner, make for an ideal out-of-season afternoon.

Even a one-day trip is feasible and enjoyable here, but there's a lot to be said for spending several days, whether in the lively coastal towns or the rustic villages of the back-country, or penetrating further inland to discover the life of the historic little cities. It's a region of vast undulating fields, interspersed with pretty wooded valleys. There's been a lot of industrial development in places, yet this sits side by side with surprisingly rustic countryside. Many of the towns are dominated by a beautiful Gothic cathedral, Gothic architecture having developed early here. Some of the oldest and best examples of the style can be found in these north-western towns, ranging from the first attempts in the cathedrals of Laon and Noyon to the full-blown Gothic masterpiece of Amiens.

Historically there have always been close links with England. For over 200 years, right into the 16th century, the town of Calais belonged to the English crown, a last remnant of the period when the whole of western France was ruled by England's Plantagenet kings. And of course, the many neat, well-tended little Commonwealth war cemeteries in this area are a reminder that this part of France was the battlefield of western Europe in two world wars. In fact, generations of English (and later, British) soldiers have fought here, sometimes against the French (as in the Hundred Years War) and sometimes with the French (in the First and Second World Wars).

This is not really one region, but two: Picardy and Flanders. Indeed, between them, there is a third: Artois. These old names correspond roughly to the present-day départements: Flanders is Nord, Artois is Pas-de-Calais, and Picardy now encompasses the Somme, Oise and Aisne départements.

At the very top of France, close to the Belgian border, is French Flanders (Flandres, in French). In fact, Flanders extends from here, through Belgium, right into the Netherlands, and during the Middle Ages this was a wealthy, powerful nation, forging alliances and treaties which served to protect and enrich it. Gradually, Flanders was broken up into the separate states which we see today.

Over the centuries, the Flemish were often in opposition to France, and they still have characteristics and customs which mark them out as different from the other French. Over the border in Belgium and Holland, the Flemish language has survived virtually intact, but even in French Flanders there's an accent and a *patois* which originate with the old language. The architecture – not the new estates of brick dwellings, but the grander civic buildings – has a distinctly Flemish style: town halls tend to be extremely ornate and often have a large belfry; churches are spacious; older houses are tall and elaborately gabled; and many of the towns and villages have a curious clock-tower, another Flemish custom.

If you're here at the right moment, you may come across one of the popular Giant Festivals – Fêtes des Géants – held in the towns and villages of French Flanders. Huge models, normally one of a man and one of a woman, though sometimes of a whole family, all dressed in traditional local costume, are brought out of storage and lead a big procession round town. The atmosphere is somehow both solemn and merry, and most of the local residents take part.

Picardy (Picardie, in French) is a different story altogether and, despite a certain cultural overlap with Flanders, is quite French in history and character. Nowadays the name also tends to encompass the old region of Artois, the band of slightly hillier terrain lying between Arras and the coast. The Picardy countryside is not as flat as in Flanders; on the whole there's less industry, and the older buildings tend to be made of stone rather than brick. Picardy is also surprisingly large, reaching right across from Boulogne almost to Reims, the capital of Champagne, 250 km away. There's plenty to see, plenty to eat, plenty to enjoy.

À table

Though much influenced by the rest of France, northerners like strong-flavoured, rich, meaty food and plenty of it. To some extent, they are particularly fond of the very things which most Britons *don't* like: tripe, offal, spicy pâtés and acrid, ultra-strong cheeses. Some of the cheeses are so strong-smelling it's considered something of a joke even among local people; one variety, made of Maroilles mixed with pepper and herbs and then allowed to ferment for months, is actually called Vieux Puant (literally, Old Stinker). In polite company it's known as Béthune. Curiously, though, while undoubtedly some do have a pretty powerful flavour, they're all much milder on the tongue than on the nose.

The Flemish have their own culinary traditions and are very fond of sausages, particularly *andouillettes* (tripe sausage), while hearty stews are a speciality, especially *hochepot*, which, as the name suggests, is a hot-pot of meat and vegetables. You'll see signs on bakeries and restaurant windows offering *flamiches*, vegetable tart with cream, and *flamiche au Maroilles*, a tart of Maroilles cheese which is typically Flemish. Picardy enjoys its stews, too. *Soupe des hortillons* is a substantial vegetable stew, appropriate in an area noted for its huge fields of carrots, cabbages and cauliflower. A curiosity of the Picard and Flemish cuisine is that beer is often an ingredient in the local dishes; *carbonade flamande*, for example, is beef braised with beer. Unlike most of the French, northerners are great beer-drinkers, and great beer-makers, too. You should certainly try the local brews, available in any supermarket or food store: they're palatable and inexpensive, and have quite a kick to them.

CALAIS
Ferry port

First sight of France for millions of holiday-makers each year, Calais is bright and bustling and has some excellent shops. Beyond that, however, its attractions are limited. Although dating back to the Middle Ages, the town has almost nothing to show for its age. For much of its history Calais was in English hands, being the last fragment of French soil to be lost in the long struggle between the English and French monarchs. It was in 1558 that France finally recaptured the town, leaving Mary Tudor so bereft that she declared: 'When I am dead and opened, you shall find "Calais" lying in my heart.' The English influence

remained, though: the town has the only church in all France
built in English Perpendicular style; and the great lacemaking
factories which made the town prosperous in the 19th century
were largely owned and worked by English residents. Even
now, the large number of British visitors help Calais to keep its
reputation as 'the most English town in France'. Unfortunately,
it was almost entirely destroyed during the Second World War,
and has been reconstructed in a modern, charmless style.

Originally, Calais was that small part of town which is gathered close to the port. Entirely surrounded by water (with the
Channel on one side, and canals all round), this older quarter is
almost like an island. Today the district is called **Calais-Nord**,
and this is where the best hotels and restaurants are to be found.
The focal point of Calais-Nord is the large and bleak market
square called Place d'Armes. At one end of the square rises one
of the only relics of the town's past, a gaunt 13th-century brick
watchtower called Tour de Guet.

Rue Royale runs up from Place d'Armes to Pont Georges-V,
the bridge across the canal to the sprawling newer part of town,
known as **Calais-Sud**. (Just across the bridge is the railway
station on one side of the road and the Calais tourist office on
the other.) It is in this larger southern part of town that most of
the real life of Calais takes place. Standing between the two
districts is an unmissable landmark, the gaudily ornate Flemish-
style town hall, with its distinctive orange clockface. This eye-
catching building is not as old as it looks; although in medieval
Flemish style, it dates back only to the early years of this
century. In front of it is Rodin's 'Monument to the Burghers of
Calais', which recalls the six notable citizens who offered their
own lives if Edward III, who was besieging the place, would
spare the rest of the town's population. Impressed by their
fortitude, Edward allowed the six burghers to live – and all the
other citizens of Calais as well.

Opposite the town hall, in Parc St Pierre, there's an unusual
museum, Musée de la Guerre (Museum of the War), dedicated
mainly to recalling the period of the Nazi occupation. Another
museum close by is the Musée des Beaux-Arts (Fine Arts
Museum) beside Parc Richelieu on the other side of the canal.

Town Hall at Calais

Here you'll find displays of sculpture and painting from the 16th to the 20th centuries, as well as a room devoted to the history of lacemaking.

The main shopping district, and the centre of town, is along busy Boulevard Jacquard and round the corner into Boulevard Lafayette. Along both roads there are fine pâtisseries, charcuteries and other good shops, together with useful department stores. If you'd prefer to find everything under a single roof, the largest hypermarket is the Mammouth Centre Commercial (Mon.–Sat. 9 a.m.–9.30/10 p.m.), ten minutes from town along the Boulogne road (N1). As well as a huge supermarket, it has many smaller specialist shops, and there are reasonable places to have a meal while you're there.

BOULOGNE

Ferry port

By far the most appealing of the short-crossing Channel ports, Boulogne rises from a lively modern area close to the harbour at the mouth of the river Liane, up to a handsome older quarter enclosed by impressive ramparts. The newer, lower town is called the Ville Basse, while the walled upper town is the Haute Ville. In the 19th and early 20th centuries the Ville Basse was popular with English ladies and gentlemen who had fallen somewhat from grace at home. Perhaps they had married without family approval, or lost some of their fortune, and decided to live in this congenial waterside town almost within sight of their native land. The picturesque Ville Basse was destroyed during the Second World War, and rebuilt in a functional modern style. Unusually, however, this does not detract from its charm. Boulogne today is also a huge fishing port with quite extensive industrial areas, yet these are completely hidden away on the far side of the river Liane, and as a result 'visitor's Boulogne' feels like quite a small place.

The main streets form something like a little rectangle, with Rue Thiers and Rue Victor Hugo on two sides, and short sections of Grande Rue and Rue Faidherbe along the other two sides. In this compact area the pavements are always crowded with pedestrians, giving an agreeable bustling air. There are many brasseries and inexpensive restaurants, and you'll find several excellent shops. Look out for style and quality, not just bargains. Among the best known of the specialist food stores is the traditional cheese specialist Olivier in Rue Thiers, which supplies a number of prestigious British restaurants.

The main square of the lower town is Place Dalton, in front of Église St Nicholas. All around it are moderately priced establishments ideal for a drink, a snack or a meal. The best of them, in my view, is **Chez Jules**. This popular brasserie can provide a reasonably good meal at any time of day. On Wednesday and Saturday mornings the square is filled to bursting with market stalls loaded with excellent fresh local produce. Country people come into town to sell their small amounts of herbs, rabbits, chickens, flowers, eggs and farm-made cheese. The scene is provincial and old-fashioned, particularly on Wednesdays. If it's fish and seafood you want, the place to buy is on the quayside every morning, when fishermen and their wives sell the fresh catch.

From Place Dalton, make your way up the hill to the Haute Ville, which luckily escaped damage during the last war. The substantial walls of the old town preserve a quiet atmosphere in its narrow lanes. Many of the buildings have been well restored by an organization called Renaissance du Vieux Boulogne, who give guided tours. Along the top of the ramparts is a broad leafy walkway overlooking the rest of Boulogne and the sea, and giving the best view of Boulogne's 13th-century château. It takes about half an hour to go all the way round the town walls.

Despite the latter-day importance of neighbouring Calais, it is Boulogne's Haute Ville which has by far the longer history. The fortifications themselves were reconstructed in 1231 on Roman foundations. From the heights of old Boulogne, Julius Caesar gazed towards Britannia and prepared his great invasion fleet, which set sail in 55 BC (although the conquest of Britain was not successfully achieved until some 100 years later). In 1803 Napoleon almost re-enacted the event, basing himself 3 km out of town, where he erected the Colonne de la Grande Armée with a rather absurd statue of himself in Roman garb, staring towards the English coast. It was rendered even more absurd by having its head shot off by the British navy during the last war. For two years Napoleon enlarged the harbour at Boulogne and filled it with ships ready for the invasion, but then came the Battle of Trafalgar, and difficulties with his forces in Austria, so the British project was abandoned.

The Cathédrale de Notre Dame, beneath a dark Italianate dome, dominates Boulogne from its site in the Haute Ville. It is a curious structure, designed and built over a period of forty years (1827–66) by the local priest, who had no architectural knowledge and paid for the work by public subscriptions. In its crypt are intriguing remains, with mosaics and frescoes, of an older church and a Roman temple to Diana. Among the other notable buildings within the walled town are the brick-and-stone town hall (18th century), which backs on to the Gothic belfry (12th and 13th centuries); the Annociades convent (17th century), containing a library; and several fine private mansions of the early 19th century.

For a moment's rest with coffee and pâtisserie, go to

Bethouart, near the cathedral. For a similar rest-stop in the Ville
Basse, try **Lugand** in Grande Rue. An exceptionally good
restaurant, with remarkably modest prices, is **La Matelote** (80
Boulevard Ste Beuve, tel. 21.30.17.97). The best supermarket in
town is the big Champion, in the Centre Commercial de la
Liane, where Grande Rue reaches the waterfront. This is very
convenient for anyone catching a ferry home – it's literally
minutes from the dock. For a bigger hypermarket, travel out to
Auchan (Mon.–Sat. 8 a.m.–10 p.m.), ten minutes' drive on the
St Omer road.

DUNKERQUE

Ferry port

If Dunkerque brings to mind a vast industrial port backed by
mile upon mile of oil refineries and chemical works, you're not
too far off the mark. Yet, unexpectedly, at the middle of all this
survives a likeable – even rather a charming – provincial town
in the heart of French Flanders. It has quite a lot of character,
several excellent shops, some good restaurants and relatively few
British visitors. It makes a pleasant base for a weekend in
Flanders. From here, you could even take in a trip across the
border into Belgium, just 13 km away.

For passengers arriving on the Sally Line ferry from Ramsgate,
there are still some 11 km to travel from the dock before you
reach Dunkerque (there are buses for foot passengers). The
main coast road brings you to the town's old fishing port – a
relatively easy place to park the car. From the port it's hardly
five minutes' walk to the town centre, with a pause on the way
to see the wonderfully ornate Flemish-style town hall in Place
Charles Valentin. The main streets, Rue Clémenceau and Boulevard Alexandre-III, meet in a lively central square, Place Jean
Bart, which is the heart of Dunkerque.

The main square takes its name from the native son of whom
Dunkerque is proudest, a villainous 17th-century pirate who
made a living raiding English ships. At that time, officially

sanctioned piracy – a proportion of the booty being given to the Crown – was rife upon the seven seas, and such 'official pirates' were called corsairs (or privateers). Some corsairs distinguished themselves by successfully protecting the interests, both military and commercial, of their monarch, and were sometimes paid to give protection to ships of their own country rather than attacking foreign vessels. Jean Bart of Dunkerque became one of the richest and most notorious corsairs of his day. Even so, it's surprising just how many things in the town are called after this disreputable fellow.

Dunkerque is better known to the British as the scene of a terrible rout of Allied forces by the Germans in 1940 – although it has passed into British minds as something of a victory. In May 1940 the German army swept into northern France and Belgium. With skill and determination they cut off the Allied forces, who converged upon the old harbour of Dunkerque, hoping to make their escape. The Allied leadership saw what was coming and rallied a huge flotilla of miniature vessels to dash across the Channel to save their men. They were aided by Hitler's incomprehensible order to his troops to pause before entering Dunkerque. From the harbour, and especially from the beach of neighbouring **Malo-les-Bains** (now a seaside resort), between 25 May and 4 June the Allied forces were ferried in any and every vessel, even rowing boats, that could carry them away from the French coast. The bid was successful: during those ten days, over 350,000 men managed to flee from the Germans to the safety of the British shore. The French view of events is somewhat less triumphal – they were left alone to face the mercies of the Nazi Germans. The story is told in a special display in the basement of Dunkerque's Musée Beaux-Arts (Fine Arts Museum) in Rue Clémenceau. The other floors of the museum have collections of 16th- to 20th-century Flemish and French painting. (For those who prefer modern art, the place to go is the Musée d'Art Contemporain, in a curious modern building standing among modern sculptures in gardens north of the port, between Dunkerque and Malo-les-Bains.)

At the start of Rue Clémenceau, you reach the town's two main landmarks on opposite sides of the street. The weather-beaten neo-Gothic façade of the church of St Eloi (16th century), where Jean Bart is buried, gazes across at the immense brick tower of Le Beffroi, the 15th-century belfry (which has the tourist office on the ground floor).

For a sit-down and a coffee, go to the youthful, fashionable, popular brasserie **Le Grand Morien**, in Place Jean Bart. There are temptations in and around the square for anyone who's thinking of buying treats to take home. Boutteau is a *salon de thé* selling luxurious cakes and chocolates. In Rue du Président Poincaré, leading off the square, Crémerie La Ferme has whole rounds of Dutch cheese, Brie de Meaux and Raclette. Pâtisseries Poulain is another tempting chocolatier with exquisite hand-made delicacies. Le Manoir is the town's best *épicerie fine*, with a particularly good range of Flemish produce. For those who prefer a trip out to the hypermarket, the Carrefour (Mon.–Sat. 9 a.m.–9 p.m.) is ten minutes from town, and Auchan (Mon.–Fri. 9 a.m.–10 p.m., Sat. 8 a.m.–10 p.m.) is five minutes from the ferry port.

Most hotel accommodation in Dunkerque is close to the old harbour and geared to the business traveller. Smaller, more homely and inexpensive hotels can be found not far from the beach in pleasant Malo-les-Bains. My favourite restaurant in Dunkerque is **La Mer du Nord** (3 Rue du Leughenaer), near the waterside. It specializes in fish and seafood, and is a good, solid establishment of the sort which sums up all that's best about France. Everything is done with relaxed correctness, service is polite and discreet without being obsequious, and the atmosphere is quietly convivial. There are usually no English voices to be heard.

DOWN THE COAST

The stretch of coast from Calais to Boulogne (*about 45 km by road*) is bright and airy, with lovely sea views from high white cliffs; it's evocatively known as the **Côte d'Opale**, the Opal Coast.

The road to take is D940. Soon after leaving Calais it passes through the little beach resort of **Blériot-Plage**, named after the pioneer aviator Louis Blériot, who flew across the Channel in a half-hour flight on 25 July 1909. The exact spot is marked by a monument 500 metres west of the town. The sandy beach continues to the **Channel Tunnel** entrance at Sangatte. Soon after, there's another monument to a pioneer airman, Latham, but his early Channel attempt from this spot in 1909 was unsuccessful. The road climbs up the imposing chalk cliffs to wild and windswept **Cap Blanc-Nez** (literally, White Nose Cape), which looks loftily along the shore back to Calais, and across the Channel to the equally impressive white line of the Kent coast 20 miles away. The sandy beach continues, backed by dunes in places, past the picturesque seashore village of **Wissant** (the name is Flemish for 'white sand'). Turn right just after Audinghen to reach **Cap Gris-Nez** (Grey Nose Cape), not so high as Blanc-Nez but even closer to the British shore.

Turning towards Boulogne, the coast road passes through appealing **Ambleteuse**, with its Roman remains and sturdy fortress, to more stately **Wimereux**. Ferries and hovercraft pass very close to the beach at this point, yet the place retains its civilized, well-bred feeling. **Hôtel de l'Atlantique** (Digue de Mer, tel. 21.32.41.01), on the waterfront, is a good unpretentious hotel with an enjoyable restaurant specializing, not surprisingly, in fish dishes. It was from Wimereux that Marconi made the first radio link across the Channel. In the local cemetery lies the grave of Colonel John Macrae, poet of the Great War, who wrote: 'In Flanders fields the poppies grow/Between the crosses, row on row.'

Another couple of kilometres brings you into **Boulogne** (see p. 21), after which D940 continues southward, but no longer beside the sea. Turn right, off the road, to visit **Hardelot-Plage**. This neat and tidy old-fashioned resort, once rather grand, lies among woods and dunes. Charles Dickens used often to come here with his friend Ellen Ternan. Travel another 15 km to pretty but busy **Étaples**, at the mouth of the river Canche. The Commonwealth war cemetery here is one of the largest burial grounds in Europe.

Cross the Canche in Étaples to reach the much more

distinguished, vastly more stagey resort of **Le Touquet**. Here you'll find more than mere memories of past grandeur – the place is still an exclusive resort, favoured by wealthy Parisians and English county types. Of course, not everyone in Le Touquet is of that class, and there are sometimes coach parties of noisy, beery Brits. But among the pine woods which surround the resort there are a surprising number of large and opulent villas, many of them English-owned. There are some smart hotels, too, and at Le Touquet's small airfield there is a steady stream of private planes arriving and departing. For the French market, the town's 'spa' image survives, with a thalassotherapy centre (i.e. using seawater for cures) and the obligatory casino for whiling away the hours between treatments. British visitors may prefer the golf, the promenade looking across a broad expanse of sandy beach, and the high-quality dining. One of the best restaurants, with celebratory flair and style as well as really excellent fish dishes, is **Flavio's** (Avenue du Verger, tel. 21.05.10.22).

Heading further south, D940 first reaches **Bagatelle**, a huge amusement park for families, before skirting **Berck**, an attractive and well-to-do resort with a magnificent beach. Beyond, towards the southern limits of Picardy, the coast becomes wilder with areas of marsh mixed with sand dunes on the approach to the broad estuary of the river Somme. The breezy waterside villages of **Le Crotoy** and **St Valery** (*79 km from Boulogne, 55 km from Dieppe*), one each side of the Somme bay, are delightful. This area has great importance as a bird sanctuary, a large part of it being designated the **Parc Ornithologique du Marquenterre**, signposted from the ancient village of **Rue**. You don't have to be a bird-watcher to find the place fascinating. In spring and autumn, some 350 species of birds can be sighted here – and binoculars hired from the Parc office.

JUST INLAND

Within a few minutes' drive of the ferry ports there are agreeable small country towns and villages ideal for a quick visit or a longer stay. For a couple of leisurely days out with no goal in mind other than to work up a robust appetite, the area has plenty to offer. In general, the countryside, especially in Flanders' maritime plain, is flat and consists of large fields of vegetables, generally with factory chimneys within sight, but there are also some slightly hillier, more rolling and more rustic areas, notably behind Boulogne. A feature of the more northern landscape is its network of drainage channels called *watergangs*, along which some farmers still travel by punt. And in Picardy, scattered over the whole region, there are extensive woods of oak, beech and hazel which offer tranquil walks, glorious in late autumn colours. The art of an enjoyable visit to the hinterland of Picardy and Flanders is to choose a base where you can be sure of a good dinner and a quiet night's sleep, then take in the rest of the country on leisurely drives or walks during the day.

Bergues (*21 km from Dunkerque ferry port, 9 km from Dunkerque town centre*) is a small fortified town of considerable charm. Its defences, constructed by Vauban (for Louis XIV), combine sturdy walls with an outer ring of canal-moats. Going through one of the four fine gateways, within the walls you find cobbled streets and several handsome buildings in 16th-century Flemish style – town hall, belfry and flower-decked houses.

St Omer (*40 km from Dunkerque ferry, 40 km from Calais, 53 km from Boulogne*), a bigger town, manages to hang on to its Flemish atmosphere, with a pedestrianized old quarter, many attractive mansions two or three centuries old and some stately public buildings. Take a look in and around the main square, Place Foch, where you'll find the elaborate town hall (tourist office inside), the Ancien Bailliage (now the national savings bank Caisse d'Épargne) and the Hôtel Sandelin (now housing a good collection of medieval Flemish art and crafts). The other great landmark is the 13th-century Gothic basilica of Notre-Dame, tucked away in a quiet square. Huge inside, it contains much good sculpture and, perhaps more interestingly, an astronomical clock dated 1558. Spacious public gardens cover the site of the old city ramparts. From here there's a wide view across the fields of Flanders. Just outside town to the east, the **Forêt de Rihoult-Clairmarais** is a pleasant, popular area for walks and picnics under the old oaks.

Cassel (*40 km from Dunkerque ferry port*) is a quiet old town which rises surprisingly high above the Flemish flatlands all around. Quiet, that is, except for three colourful and traditional festival days: the first Sunday in March, when the town's 'Giant' Reuze-Papa is on parade; Easter Monday, when the 'Giant' wife Reuze-Maman also comes out for the day (the 'Giants' are huge lightweight models in old-fashioned attire which are pushed along at the head of a big procession); and Fête de la St Jean, the lively summer solstice fair on 24 June. Cassel's central square, Grand' Place, is surrounded by imposing steep-roofed houses with dormer windows, in the Flemish style. Some are especially striking, such as the 16th-century Hôtel de la Noble Cour with its carved stone façade (inside, there's a local museum). Beside the square, Notre-Dame church is a fine example of Flemish Gothic. Narrow back-streets climb, sometimes in steps, to the very summit of the hill, where an 18th-century windmill stands in public gardens. The view is glorious, and indeed from this spot Marshal Foch, commander of the French during the First World War, directed his forces during 1914 and 1915. From here, so the saying goes, you can see five kingdoms: 'France, Belgium, Holland, England and the kingdom of God.' I was up there on the clearest of clear days, yet still could not make out three of those places!

Ardres (*17 km from Calais*), between St Omer and Calais, has some pretty old houses and is well placed for inland exploring. Just 6 km from Ardres, on the road to Guînes, is the site of the Field of the Cloth of Gold where in 1520 Henry VIII and François I met in rival splendour to discuss the irritating matter of England's title to this whole region of France. Today it's just a ploughed field of vegetables. Almost next to it is the Forêt de Guînes, lovely woods with easy-to-follow footpaths. The **Grand Hôtel Clément** (91 Esplanade du Maréchal-Leclerc, tel. 21.82.25.25) at Ardres is a pleasant hotel, a member of the Relais de Silence (hotels in quiet locations), and serves the most marvellous food.

Desvres (*19 km from Boulogne*) is a small lively town with a busy Tuesday-morning market. While here, search out the fine porcelain and pottery for which it has long been noted. Each

November, Desvres has one of the more unusual local festivals, being dedicated to custard pies. However, in France, these are not for throwing at people, but for eating. Just north there's the Forêt de Desvres, almost 3,000 acres, a popular area for picnics and walks; west lies the even larger Forêt de Boulogne; while a lovely drive southward from Desvres down the pretty little **valley of the river Course** brings you to **Montreuil** (see below).

MONTREUIL

38 km from Boulogne

The lofty little fortified town of **Montreuil-sur-Mer**, the setting for Victor Hugo's *Les Misérables*, was a seaport in Roman times but now, thanks to almost incredible alluvial changes along the shoreline, stands atop a hill some 15 km inland from Le Touquet. On top of its massive grass-covered fortifications there's a footpath with a commanding view over the undulating country-side. The 'old' upper part of Montreuil, including the ramparts, has all been built since the destruction of the earlier city by Charles V in 1537. In the main square, there's the Flamboyant Gothic chapel of the Hôtel-Dieu hospital, which has a tremendously ornate exterior but is tiny inside, with good stained glass and fine-carved wooden panelling. Standing opposite is the church of St Saulve, originally 11th century, but extensively repaired after war damage many times in its history, including twice in this century.

Parts of the imposing Citadelle, a separate fortress within the city walls, date from the 11th and 13th centuries. Protected by a (now empty) moat and an entrance gate flanked by two powerful towers, the Citadelle is overgrown and unrestored, a strange, rather eerie place with subterranean casemates and 'Queen Berthe's Tower' in which are recorded the coats of arms of thousands of noblemen killed by the English in 1415 at nearby Agincourt (present-day **Azincourt**, not far off to the east).

Hôtel-Restaurant le Darnetal (Place Darnetal, tel. 21.06.04.87) is friendly and unpretentious, with modestly priced menus. Close by, the beautiful old **Château de Montreuil** (4 Chaussée des Capucins, tel. 21.81.53.04), standing in private gardens, is a luxurious Relais et Châteaux hotel with a first-class restaurant specializing in light, fresh cooking inspired by traditional local specialities.

LILLE

65 km from Dunkerque ferry

Although an industrial centre, Lille has plenty to recommend it for a short break. It's the nearest major French city to British shores, and has urban pleasures to offer: entertainment, dining, culture, shopping. At its centre there's a bustling old quarter with some impressive remnants of a grand past. Despite the size of the city, everything of note is within a walkable area. Especially worth seeing are the narrow back-streets of what's called Le Vieux Lille, around the 12th-century Hospice Comtesse; the huge Porte de Paris of 1682; the mighty Citadelle built by Vauban to guard this frontier town (it's considered one of the finest examples of his work); and several extremely ornate Flemish Baroque buildings like the 17th-century Ancienne Bourse and the 15th-century Palais Rihour (with tourist office). Most astonishing is the late 19th-century Théâtre de l'Opéra, on which statuary seems to be climbing right out of the walls. The city's large Musée Beaux-Arts (Fine Arts Museum), in Place de la République, has what is regarded as one of the best collections of Flemish and northern French painters, and is very instructively laid out.

As a frontier city, Lille suffered enormously over the centuries, changing hands from Burgundians (15th century) to Spanish (16th) to French (17th). During the First World War it remained in German hands for almost the whole period of the conflict, while in the Second World War it was bombed continuously from 1940 to 1944. Surprisingly, it survives. The people have a level-headed and hard-working reputation, and among themselves speak a curious French Flemish dialect of their own.

If you visit Lille as a tourist (rather than on business), it's important to stay in the centre. There are plenty of cheap hotels around the rather rough railway station area. For something better, and accordingly pricier, there are several possibilities around the central Grand Place. Several of Lille's restaurants have high reputations: among the great names are **Le Restaurant** (Place Sebastopol, tel. 20.57.05.05), **Le Flambard** (79 Rue Angleterre, tel. 20.51.00.06) and **À l'Huître** (3 Rue Chats-Bossus, tel. 20.55.43.41).

AMIENS AND THE BATTLEFIELDS

129 km from Boulogne, 115 km from Dieppe

The one really outstanding thing about Amiens is its Cathédrale Notre-Dame. A masterpiece of Gothic art, built in the 13th century, it is a triumph of design and the medieval stonemason's craft. The exterior is an intricate wealth of carving, with three deep doorways surmounted by two towers of unequal height. Inside, the soaring nave is the longest in France. There's fine wood-carving, too, and you'll see memorials to soldiers who died in the surrounding countryside, among them '600,000 men of the armies of Britain and Ireland'. During the heavy bombardments of the First World War, the cathedral was draped in sandbags, which proved remarkably effective – it sustained little damage. Fortunately, a few of the town's older civic buildings in this quarter also managed to escape serious harm, but on the whole Amiens is noisy, crowded and industrial, having been almost destroyed in both wars. Quartier St Leu is its small surviving medieval district. Another point of interest for art enthusiasts is the Musée de Picardie (in Rue de la République), which has collections of some good Flemish painting. Boulevard Jules Verne, lying just south of the perimeter of the central quarter, was renamed in honour of the author (1828–1905) who moved here from Nantes and spent most of his life living in this street: the house has been turned into the Jules Verne

Documentation Centre, where you can learn more about the writer and his times.

Beginning on the fringes of the town, and extending away into the flat countryside, are the *hortillonages*, a large area of reclaimed fields separated by canals on which the more old-fashioned farmers still travel in punts.

The country north and east of Amiens was the scene of some of the worst slaughter of the First World War, and is dotted with neat Commonwealth war cemeteries, still carefully tended. There's a marked route called Circuit de Souvenir which takes you to the principal memorials and battle sites. Details of the itinerary can be picked up at any local tourist office, for example in Amiens at Maison de la Culture, 1 Rue Jean Catelas. The route begins at **Albert** (*28 km from Amiens*), which has its own tourist office at 4 Rue Gambetta. Just beyond Albert is **La Boisselle**, where the Front was formed in 1914. The Battle of the Somme started here on 1 July 1916. On the Circuit, one of the first places reached is the **Beaumont-Hamel Newfoundland Memorial**, a part of the original unaltered battlefield on land which has been given in perpetuity to the Canadian government. The ground is cut with tortuous trenches and cramped dug-outs, and marked by mortar craters.

Arras, at the end of the marked itinerary, was faithfully reconstructed after both wars. The centre of town is made up by two huge squares lined with handsome tall buildings ornately gabled in the Flemish way and arcaded at street level. The larger square is the incredibly vast Grande Place, with the so-called Petit Place or Place des Héros adjoining on its south-west corner. The smaller square contains a superb town hall rebuilt in its original ornate 16th-century style, which amply demonstrates the prosperity of the town in that period. For centuries, Arras was synonymous with fine cloth and richly decorated tapestries, but that industry has now died out.

Markets fill both squares on Wednesday and Saturday mornings. Underneath the cobble-stones there's an extraordinary underground network of vaulted rooms and passageways called Les Souterrains or Les Boves; they're entered from the town hall, and were used for over 1,000 years to provide wartime protection for the citizens. Poor Arras has seen more than its share

Market Square at Arras

of fighting and bloodshed. It was Robespierre's native town, which did not prevent him from having a guillotine erected in Place du Théâtre. The Arras Memorial to the Missing records the names of almost 36,000 men whose bodies were not found after First World War battles in this area, while the Mur des Fusillés (literally, Wall of the Shot) is where 200 French Resistance members were executed by German firing squads in the Second World War.

Eight kilometres north of Arras, **Vimy Ridge** was one of the worst battlefields of the Great War, with fighting from 1914 to 1917. A total of about 425,000 Canadians took part in the First World War, and 60,000 of them died in a single battle at Vimy Ridge on 9 and 10 April 1917. The bodies of 11,000 of them were never recovered. After the Armistice, the land was given to the Canadian government. Part has been maintained exactly as it was in 1919, complete with trenches, craters and tunnels, while another part is being allowed to erode in the wind and rain. On top of the ridge itself (Hill 145, as it was known during the war) rises an impressive monument, tall, distinctive and sombre, looking down on to a landscape blighted not by war but by industry. Less than 5 km away is Notre-Dame de Lorette, the French national memorial and cemetery.

COMPIÈGNE AND AROUND

216 km from Calais by autoroute

The main attraction of popular Compiègne is the curious triangular Royal Palace and its serene Petit Parc, backing on to the

Compiègne forest. The site having been a royal hunting ground for centuries, the present imposing palace was constructed in the 18th century. Here Louis XVI's queen Marie-Antoinette ('Let them eat cake') lived in splendour, while no sooner was the Revolution over than Napoleon installed himself here in similar style, later to be followed by Napoleon III. Their ostentatious *appartements*, complete with tasteless – if priceless – furniture, can be visited on guided tours. Included on the tour is the interesting Musée Nationale de la Voiture et du Tourisme, with early vehicles, which occupies part of the palace.

In fact, though, Compiègne's real attractions are its civilized atmosphere, the wonderful forest with its long paths for walking or cycling, and the river Oise. The town rises from the left bank, but on both sides of the river there are handsome embankment walks. The town centre, though crowded, has several picturesque old mansions, as well as many top-quality specialist food shops. The most distinctive of the historic buildings is the medieval town hall in Place de l'Hôtel de Ville. The façade is a riot of statuary, among which you can see Louis XII and Joan of Arc who was captured here in 1430 by the Burgundians and handed over to their English allies. Above all there are the animated little figures, called *picantins*, who ring out the hours. The town hall houses a rare collection of metal toy soldiers, formed into really quite surprising colourful re-enactments of great moments in French history. Next door, the Musée Vivenel is Compiègne's municipal museum, noted for a good collection of classical Greek vases. Every Saturday, Place de l'Hôtel de Ville is taken over by a lively market.

There are many hotels to choose from in and around town. On the right bank are some reliable solid establishments in the middle price range. A few paces from the main square, **Hôtel de France** (17 Rue Floquet, tel. 44.40.02.74) is a 17th-century inn with fairly simple rooms but an excellent restaurant. For a coffee break, I like pâtissier-chocolatier **Moreau** in Place de l'Hôtel de Ville.

The river Oise forms the western limit of old Compiègne, but on every other side the town is enclosed by the oak and beech woods of the **Forêt de Compiègne**. Avenue Royale (beside the château) takes you into the forest, following it through the château's Grand Parc. The **Beaux-Monts**, soon reached, are delightful wooded hills crossed by a twisting lane. On the far side they slope down towards the banks of the river Aisne. In a forest clearing near the Aisne, the **Clairière de l'Armistice** (Armistice Clearing) is the place where, in Marshal Foch's private railway carriage, the Armistice was signed on 11 November 1918 at the end of the Great War. The carriage now standing in the clearing is an exact replica of Marshal Foch's original. The massive fortified château at pretty **Pierrefonds** marks the eastern edge of the Forêt. Originally built in 1407, the castle was used as an away-from-it-all retreat by Napoleon, and then in 1857 was almost completely rebuilt for Napoleon III.

On the other side of the Aisne, more forests follow the bank of the Oise as far as **Noyon** (*24 km from Compiègne, 207 km from Boulogne*), which was a Celtic and then a Roman town, and it was here that Charlemagne was crowned king of the Franks in 768. Noyon doesn't seem so important now, but thanks to its distinguished past there's plenty to see. For some 900 years it has been dominated by a magnificent cathedral, the first in France to be built in Gothic style. The cool, pale interior, with three aisles and three storeys of arches, has great elegance. Behind the cathedral there's an exquisite little 16th-century *bibliothèque* (library) constructed entirely of wood, while a few paces away the 15th-century town hall is one of the finest medieval civic buildings in France. The early Protestant, Jean Calvin, was born in the town in 1509, and lived here to the age of 11; however, the 'Birthplace of Calvin' in Place Aristide Briand, with a museum dedicated to the religious reformer, was not built until 1927! There's a big, lively produce market in Place de l'Hôtel de Ville every Saturday morning; while on the first Tuesday in each month the huge Marché Franc cattle market fills the whole town centre, as it has done for centuries.

CHANTILLY AND SENLIS

240 km from Calais by autoroute

Though much of the riverside itself is industrialized, the lower Oise valley benefits from the succession of fine woodlands close to its left bank, especially the large, peaceful Forêts of Halatte, Chantilly and, further east, Ermenonville.

Well placed at the meeting point of all three forests, **Senlis** is a busy town with a great deal of medieval character. A considerable section of ancient Gallo-Roman ramparts still encloses the old centre, where there are narrow historic streets and attractive old buildings. The 12th-century former cathedral was, like others in this region, among Europe's first great Gothic structures. Almost opposite, Hôtel des Trois-Pots conceals a 13th-century mansion behind a 16th-century façade. In the Middle Ages the town grew considerably beyond the ancient walls, and eventually new defences were built at a greater distance from the centre. These have now largely been replaced by the encircling boulevards, though a fragment of the fortifications survives down by the river Nonette. Beyond, there is a ruined Roman arena.

Ermenonville, on the far side of its forest, stands on unusually sandy soil, and the barren area just before town is known as Le Désert. There's even a weird 'Mer de Sable' – sea of sand – which is part of an amusement park. Another much more grandiose entertainment area on the edge of the forest, and only about 8 km from the town, is the immense (383 acres) **Parc Astérix**, where the zany world of the Astérix comics comes to life. You don't have to be a child to enjoy it, although it does help; 86 per cent of French people aged between 15 *and 50* have read all or most of the Astérix comic books. The humour, which is based on a slapstick version of the wars between the Romans and the Gauls, is actually quite adult, and involves many clever French puns. Parts of the Parc are devoted to other historical set-pieces, like the Rue de Paris, which illustrates 1,000 years of history in the capital.

Jean-Jacques Rousseau, the radical philosopher and writer, died at Ermenonville in 1778 while visiting the town's château as a guest. He was buried on an island in a lake within the château's park, but his body was later moved to the Panthéon in Paris.

In the other direction from Senlis, **Chantilly** is France's racing capital. It's in a fine forest setting, with a handsome lakeside château, in fact two châteaux (Grand and Petit) which are linked. The excellent Musée Condé, inside the building, contains portraits, fine 17th-century tapestries and superb examples of illuminated 14th–16th-century manuscripts, including one of the very finest, Les Très Riches Heures du Duc de Berry. The château has magnificent 18th-century royal stables, Les Grandes-Écuries, where the horses lived in a setting as grand as anything built for their owners. The name Chantilly brings to mind not just racing but also a kind of lace (black or white silk lace of delicate floral pattern) and a kind of cream (whipped with sugar), both of which were invented here, though neither is any longer especially associated with the town.

Catering to many prosperous visitors, Chantilly has several first-class restaurants, such as the **Relais du Coq Chantant** (21 Route de Creil, tel. 44.57.01.28), and good hotels. For somewhere special, stay in forest seclusion at the wonderful **Hostellerie du Lys** (63 7eme -Avenue, Lys-Chantilly, tel. 44.21.26.19).

ST QUENTIN AND LAON

From Calais to St Quentin: 160 km; to Laon: 200 km

A historic town, once enclosed with mighty ramparts, **St Quentin** rises from the right bank of the river Somme. The ramparts have gone now – except for a remnant in a pleasant park – to be replaced by busy boulevards. In the last few years the town has spread far beyond its ancient limits. It suffered enormous damage during the wars, and subsequent rebuilding has given the place a rather characterless modern appearance, but the greatest of its historic buildings have been carefully repaired and restored.

The two finest survivors of old St Quentin are the flamboyant town hall in the central Place, and the great medieval Gothic cathedral (or basilica) nearby. Much of the town centre between these two landmarks has been made traffic free. A few paces to the north in Rue Antoine Lécuyer is the Musée Lécuyer, with local arts and antiquities, the most outstanding of which is the large collection of pastels by the distinguished 18th-century portraitist Quentin Delatour (or La Tour, as he is sometimes known), who was a native of St Quentin.

Either on the route nationale (N44) or on the autoroute, it's a fast run across the wide fields to the other side of the Somme to reach **Laon**, one of Picardy's most interesting and attractive towns. It can be seen from afar, perched on top of a curious hill which rises startlingly from an almost flat landscape of broad farmland. The striking setting has been aptly called *la montagne couronnée*, the crowned mountain. It's the old part of town, the Ville Haute, which stands on the high ground; the newer districts, or Ville Basse, cluster around the foot of the hill.

Laon was originally a powerful settlement of the Gauls, conquered and taken over by the Romans, who fortified it, enlarged it – and were driven out in their turn by the Franks, one of the indomitable 'Germanic tribes' who gave the Romans such trouble. The Franks were destined to become the French nobility, but in the early days took control only of this region of Picardy. Subsequently Laon became a royal residence, and for over 1,200 years, from AD 497 onwards, was the seat of one of the most important bishoprics in France.

During the Hundred Years War, the Religious Wars and, especially, the 20th century, Laon took the brunt of some fierce fighting and destruction. Yet curiously enough, it has come through with a great deal of character and charm. The shape of the high ground divides the Ville Haute into two separate districts. Both of them, bound within encircling ramparts, are picturesque and interesting.

The older half of the Ville Haute is called La Cité, with a lovely cathedral at its centre. Dating from the middle of the 12th century, this is one of the oldest Gothic churches in France, and combines Gothic elegance with the sturdy simplicity of the Romanesque style. Pause to admire the ornate façade, then wander inside the tall, pale interior of this beautiful building. Of course, Laon was in the midst of the battlefields of the First World War, and in the cathedral there's a plaque poignantly dedicated to the memory of 'One million dead of the British Empire who fell in the Great War'.

Laon Cathedral

Place du Général Leclerc, adjacent to the town hall, is the main square where La Cité meets the other half of the Ville Haute, called Le Bourg. The Bourg's handsome church of St Martin is even older than the cathedral, dating back to 1150, and is much more in the awkward stage of the transition between Romanesque and Gothic.

Stroll on the ramparts and among the back-streets. Linger over a meal at one of several decent restaurants. There's a quirky little museum at 32 Rue Georges-Ermant, with an odd collection of classical statues and vases, archaeological finds and paintings by northern artists; in the grounds, there's a small octagonal temple of the Knights Templar. It's almost bare inside, except for memories and mystery which still hang in the cool air.

Hôtel les Chevaliers (3 Rue Serurier, tel. 23.23.43.78) is a modest and fairly inexpensive hotel and restaurant in the Ville Haute; it's attractive, with beams and sturdy walls. Most of the cheaper, more everyday places are in the modern districts at the bottom of the hill.

West of Laon, the forests of St Gobain and of Coucy make up a single extensive area of pleasant wooded country. Here you'll find some massive old oaks, three former monasteries and the last remnant of the **Château de Coucy**, a 13th-century hilltop castle once legendary for its huge size. Throughout the Middle Ages it was one of medieval Europe's most awesome and best-known fortresses. The proud Lords of Coucy proclaimed in their family motto: 'Roi ne suys, ni prince, ni duc, ni comte aussi; je suys le Sire de Coucy' (Not king, nor prince, nor duke, nor count am I; I am Lord of Coucy). The castle was largely dismantled in 1652, and what remained was deliberately destroyed by the Germans in 1918; yet even the fragment which does survive, overlooking the village of Coucy-le-Château, still seems astonishingly large! To learn more about the castle in its heyday, and the life which was lived there, see Barbara Tuchman's book, *A Distant Mirror*.

3. CHAMPAGNE

Marne and Aube

Getting there

This region is easily reached from Calais, with an almost traffic-free autoroute (A26) direct from the ferry harbour all the way to Reims and beyond. A large number of ferries cross to Calais from Dover every day and night throughout the year (except Christmas Day). Scheduled journey times are 35 minutes on Hoverspeed's hovercraft and SeaCats, 1¼ hours on P&O and 1½ hours on Sealink. From 1993 another possibility will be to put the car on the Trans-Manche Link and head through the railway Tunnel to Sangatte, near Calais, in half an hour.

The services to Dunkerque from Ramsgate (2½ hours on Sally), and to Boulogne from Dover and Folkestone (40 minutes on Hoverspeed, 1 hour 50 minutes on Sealink), also give good access to autoroute A26.

Champagne is even closer to Dieppe (4 hours from Newhaven on Sealink), but in addition to being a longer Channel crossing, this route requires a slower drive to Champagne. The region is also hardly any further from Le Havre, on autoroutes A15, A13 and A4, than it is from Calais. However, this too involves driving on busier, slower roads, including the Périphérique around Paris, and takes at least an hour longer than the journey from Calais.

CHAMPAGNE has a great deal to recommend it for a short break. Though so accessible, it's thoroughly French, thoroughly satisfying and full of atmosphere, with pleasing, neat-looking productive countryside and some attractive towns. For anyone with something to celebrate, surely nowhere could be more appropriate. There are hotels and restaurants perfect for a special occasion; it is preferable to stay in the country rather than in the busy towns.

One of the biggest surprises about Champagne is the lack of grape-vines! Most of the region is a patchwork of long narrow fields of cereals and green vegetables, barely undulating, sometimes almost flat. The contrast of colour between a field and its neighbours is one of the delightful features of the Champagne country. The vineyards of Champagne are mainly confined to the slopes of chalk hills just south of Reims and all around Épernay. All of this higher ground – with the exception of the

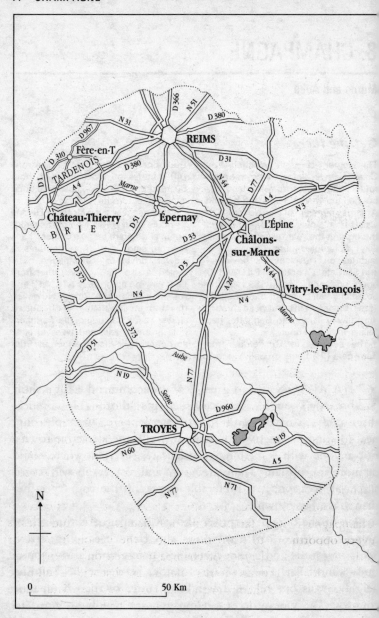

CHAMPAGNE

Champagne vineyard.

crests and summits, which are covered with forest – is densely cultivated with the tidy rows of well-kept vines clinging to wires. The entire *vignoble* (vine-growing area) of Champagne covers just 33,000 hectares, about 82,500 acres, of which some 15 per cent is fallow at any given time. Yet 250 million bottles of champagne are drunk each year. If it seems a puzzle that all the world's champagne comes from so small an area, bear in mind that less than 1½ kilos of grapes are needed to make one bottle. From the vine country, there are superb views across the rest of the Champagne region. The vineyard villages, with some exceptions, tend not to be particularly pretty; they are working communities intent upon producing one of the world's great luxuries.

Of course, whatever its other claims, the old county of Champagne is now famous only for that luxury. And there's every opportunity to learn more about the various makes (or rather, *marques*) and types of champagne even on a short visit. Many better-quality restaurants offer a wine list with a full page or two devoted to champagne alone. However, there's far more to the region than its sparkling wine. Champagne's capital, Reims, has a long and illustrious history, and deserves a visit whichever part of the region you are staying in.

In the Middle Ages the county of Champagne was always known as a place of business. For centuries it was renowned above all for big international trade fairs. From the 14th and 15th centuries onwards, the four main towns of the county as it then was – Reims, Châlons, Troyes and Provins – were already industrial, with a reputation as manufacturing centres of textiles and leather. The region fell into a certain decline as a result of the Hundred Years War, during which the Burgundians (allies of the English) attempted to take control of the county. There was more prolonged violence in the wars between Protestant and Catholic forces in the 16th and 17th centuries. In these troubled periods, the population either fled the region altogether, or moved for safety into the four main towns. The region recovered during the 18th century, but was to see yet more savage warfare. Twice in the 19th century, then again, even more damagingly, in the First World War, its broad, open plains proved ideal battlegrounds as France defended itself against invading Germans.

Not surprisingly after such a history, many of the towns retain few relics of their past. Yet even more surprising is just what does remain. Troyes preserves a considerable central area of attractive old houses, while Reims, though largely destroyed and reconstructed after the First World War, has managed to keep several distinguished buildings, including its glorious cathedral, in which almost all the monarchs of France were crowned.

À *table*

People eat well in Champagne. However, they have little in the way of a local cuisine. The air of style and luxury created by the most celebratory drink in the world has drawn in good chefs from all the surrounding regions – Burgundy, Lorraine, Flanders and the Île de France. It's in charcuterie that Champagne excels, with ham, sausages and most notably the *andouillettes* of Troyes and the pâtés and terrines *en croute* of Reims. The forests of the nearby Ardennes bring the meat of deer and boar to the tables of Champagne during the winter months, while all the year round the rivers give abundant pike, salmon and trout. The

cheese course may well include Brie, especially the great farm-
made Brie de Meaux, which comes from just outside the Champagne borders. But there are many exquisite local makes on the
cheese-board, too: gently tangy fragrant varieties, such as creamy
Chaource and firmer Langres.

The wines are of course dominated by that very symbol of
style and flamboyance: champagne. Thousands of acres of im-
maculate vineyards cover the Montagne de Reims and the Côtes
south of Épernay to produce this foaming, sparkling wine,
which comes in a huge diversity of flavours. Three types of
grapes go into making champagne: Pinot Meunier and Pinot
Noir, which are both red, and Chardonnay, which is white. Part
of the art of champagne-making is getting the mixture and
maturation right, and this is part of the skill which distinguishes
the great *marques* from the minor houses. Champagnes are known
always by the name of their producer, not as with other wines
by the name of the village, vineyard or grape variety. Interestingly, some of the best champagnes are made only with red
grapes (it's not the juice which is red, only the skins). The more
typical blend is about two-thirds red to a third white.

Nearly all the famous producers are based in Reims, Épernay
and the village of Aÿ. Their champagnes range from the extra-
sweet (*doux*), or sweet and less sweet (known curiously as *demi-
sec* and *sec*), right through to very dry (*brut*). The drier champagnes are usually drunk without food, often as an aperitif.
More 'medium' types may be drunk with every course of a meal,
although sweet champagne is best with a dessert; all are served
chilled. When ordering champagne, it may be useful to know
that *blanc de blanc* means champagne made only from white
grapes, which makes it lighter and more delicate in taste, while
crémant means a less frothy champagne.

The region also produces still wines, which have an *appellation*
of their own, called Côteaux de Champenois. Although little
known beyond the borders of the Champagne district, some of
these *champagnes naturels* are very good. They are a little lighter
than wines from neighbouring Burgundy, though there are
similarities. They are often served chilled. You will certainly
find them on local wine lists. A couple of the best still red wines

come from the nicely named village of Bouzy. It's normally a few drops of Bouzy, added to a white champagne, which makes pink champagne. A popular aperitif of the region is called *ratafia de champagne* – quite a strong drink made of local grape juice laced with *marc* (a spirit) made from champagne grapes. Unexpectedly, Champagne is also a beer region, with Châlons-sur-Marne as the main brewing centre.

REIMS

300 km from Calais, 340 km from Le Havre, 258 km from Dieppe

Although a place of importance for over 2,000 years, the capital of Champagne presents the face of a large modern city, much of it rebuilt after First World War devastation. Yet its cathedral quarter and adjacent town centre retain considerable character, and are interesting and enjoyable to visit. Reims – its name is pronounced as if the 'm' were a nasal 'n' – is closely ringed by autoroute A26; the Reims-Cathédrale exit gives easy access to this old heart of the city. There are, incidentally, plenty of parking spaces close to the cathedral.

Stand in the cobbled Place facing the cathedral's main west front and admire the deep, richly carved portals and the elaborately sculpted façade of this masterpiece of 13th-century Flamboyant Gothic architecture. Much of it has been badly damaged, and certain sculptures have been removed. Yet like a giant that could not be felled, it has a battered dignity which is inspiring. So great is the building's air of strength and magnificence that the bomb damage seems almost to enhance the impression of power. The north entrance, in Rue Robert de Coucy, is equally impressive. Stepping inside, you find that the interior of the main doorways is also heavily ornamented with carved figures. The rest of the building, though, is unadorned and colourless, almost dull, except for some fine 16th-century Flemish tapestries. Stained glass must have been its glory. Marvellous windows over the west door, in the transepts and in the radiating chapels behind the choir – although most are modern, and the best is by

Reims Cathedral

Chagall – give a glimpse of how impressive was Reims Cathedral in its heyday. In 1429 Joan of Arc held the standard of France over the head of Charles VII as he was crowned king here. Thus her prophecy was fulfilled, and soon the English were driven right out from France. The coronation of almost every king of France, from Philippe Auguste in 1180 to Charles X in 1825, took place in this cathedral.

Follow the cobbled pavement from the cathedral to the Palais de Tau next door. This former Episcopal Palace now houses the

Musée de Tau, a museum (very expensive entrance fee) preserving the cathedral's damaged statues, as well as superb medieval tapestries. In the former courtyard of the palace, you can also see new stonework which is being carved to replace the damaged sections of the cathedral.

A few paces from the cathedral, in Rue Chanzy, Musée Beaux-Arts (previously Musée St Denis) is the city's fine arts museum in grand 18th-century abbey buildings. Further along the same street is the start of the main shopping area, which extends along part of Rue Chanzy, round the corner into Rue de Vesle and into the broad Place Drouet d'Erlon.

All around the cathedral there's much to see and enjoy. Cobbled Place Royale is not a main square but a striking ensemble of stately 18th-century façades, attractively arcaded at ground level. Just beyond is Place du Forum, the site of the town's Roman forum; here you'll also find the Musée Hôtel le Vergeur, a fascinating museum of Old Reims in a restored 13th–16th-century mansion. Close by are some other interesting survivals of historic Reims, including the 16th-century Renaissance mansion Hôtel de la Salle, and the Gothic dwelling of the former Counts of Champagne, the Hôtel des Comtes de Champagne, which now belongs to the Taittinger champagne company.

Most of Reims's leading champagne houses are located either north of the centre near to the Porte de Mars, a 3rd-century Roman arch which was incorporated into the city's medieval fortifications, or south of the centre in the area beyond the Basilique St Rémi. The basilica, an 11th-century abbey church standing some 1½ km away from the cathedral quarter, is just as deserving of a visit as the cathedral itself. It's certainly an imposing building, buttressed, with many windows. Although much smaller than the cathedral, the basilica's plain and sturdy Romanesque interior has more pleasing proportions, giving a broader, more spacious feeling. Its austerity, too, is more satisfying than that of the cathedral. St Rémi is also apparently more real in the life of the town: local people pop in to pray, while on Saturdays there's one wedding after another.

Close to the basilica you can find the premises of some of the best-known names in champagne. Their extensive cellars and priceless contents may be visited, though it's often necessary to make an appointment. Champagne Veuve Cliquot-Ponsardin is housed in a handsome greenery-draped building on the busy junction at Place des Droits-de-l'Homme. Directly opposite stand the premises of Heidseick champagne, while close by are the *caves* (wine cellars) of Taittinger, Pommery and Ruinart.

Take Avenue Général Giraud, the main Châlons road leading off Place des Droits-de-l'Homme, as far as Boulevard Henry Vasnier, and you'll find one of the best hotel-restaurants in France, **Les Crayères** (64 Boulevard Henry Vasnier, tel. 26.82.80.80), set back in its park. It's an elegant mansion, a Relais et Châteaux, and is the place for a money-no-object celebration. There are many other excellent restaurants and hotels in and around the city. One of the best city-centre eating places is the grand **Le Florence** (43 Boulevard Foch, tel. 26.47.12.70), noted for its extensive list of champagnes.

ÉPERNAY

26 km from Reims

If Reims is the capital of *la* Champagne (the region), Épernay is the capital of *le* champagne (the wine). The busy little town is surrounded by vineyards, and is built upon hundreds of miles of labyrinthine *galeries*, tunnel-like cellars in which the great champagne houses make and store millions of bottles of their precious wine. The Avenue de Champagne, a main road running out from the town centre, is an amazing street lined with the imposing buildings of the *grandes marques*. The huge premises of Moët et Chandon are sufficient reminder that this company is the world's largest maker of champagne. However, 80 per cent of Moët et Chandon is exported. Very much the leader in the French market is Moët's next-door neighbour, Mercier, which exports little of its wine (the principal exception is the UK, which takes 20 per cent of Mercier's champagne).

Apart from the champagne cellars, in truth Épernay has few

other charms. The town is essentially devoted to commerce and manufacturing, and has considerable *zones industriels*.

A cellar tour: Several champagne houses welcome visitors, although at some an appointment has to be made. Perhaps the most impressive *caves* to visit are those of Champagne Mercier (76 Avenue de Champagne, tel. 26.54.71.11), where 10 guides are employed full time to take visitors on tours free of charge throughout the day. The Mercier tour is entertaining, informative and generous with the company's time and money. The huge richly carved barrel, known simply as Le Foudre (The Tun), in the Mercier entrance hall, took twenty years to make and was drawn to Paris for the 1889 Exhibition by 24 oxen and 18 horses. The trip took eight days, and the monumental barrel, made of 150 oak trees and with a capacity of 200,000 litres, has ever since been a symbol of the extravagance which the company's high-living founder Eugène Mercier made his trade mark. The visit begins with an audio-visual show, and then you are taken down to the *galeries* for a trip through the tunnels in a laser-driven train.

You will be shown the maturing bottles in their three positions designed gradually to gather the lees into the top of the bottle: first *sur lattes* (lying down), then *sur pupitre* (placed in racks at an angle like a lectern or pulpit), in which position the bottle is rotated one-sixteenth of a turn each day, and finally *sur pointe* (standing on its head). The lees are then literally frozen out, and replaced with wine sweetened or not according to whether the bottle is destined to become a *doux*, *demi-sec*, *sec* or *brut*. The maturation in Mercier's *galeries* takes anything from 1½ to 7 years, after which the champagne is sold ready to drink. It is typical of the Mercier style that several *galeries* are decorated with specially commissioned sculpture carved directly into the chalk walls. The cellars are 35 metres below ground and are a constant temperature of about 10°C – so take a sweater. At the end of the tour, visitors are invited to enjoy a complimentary glass of champagne.

For somewhere to stay or eat close to Épernay, see **Champillon** (p. 53).

THE GREAT VINEYARDS

10 km–50 km from Reims, up to about 20 km around Épernay

Épernay, 28 km south of Reims, lies at the heart of the three principal vineyard districts of Champagne. In most bottles of champagne there are grapes from all three areas.

Between Épernay and Reims rises the upland of the MON-TAGNE DE REIMS. While the summit is forested, a necklace of wine villages encircles the *montagne*, and its slopes are densely covered with vines. Follow the minor road D26 from **Mont-chenot** (11 km from Reims) right round to **Ambonnay**. On the way you pass through a succession of important wine villages, most with lovely views across the vine fields. **Chigny-les-Roses** is indeed pretty with roses; **Verzenay** produces a good local wine of its own, as does **Verzy**, beside which the Mont Sinai is the highest point on the Montagne. The beech woods here, called the **Faux de Verzy**, are 1,000 years old. At Ambonnay, turn right to reach **Bouzy**, home of the greatest of Champagne's red still wines. Follow the road through **Avenay-Val-d'Or** to **Aÿ** (pronounced Aa-ee), one of the lesser 'capitals' of champagne. Here you pass from one district to another, from the Vins de la Montagne to the Vins de la Rivière. The 'Rivière' is the VALLEY OF THE MARNE, a name perhaps better known as the scene of terrible bloodshed during the First World War.

From Aÿ turn towards Épernay, and at **Dizy** head uphill again to reach **Champillon**, a village on the border between vineyards and forest. Here the **Royal Champagne** (tel. 26.52.87.11) is an excellent hotel-restaurant with great views across the vines. Accommodation is in little self-contained bunga-lows dotted about the hotel grounds. Either on a tiny backroad, or by returning through Dizy, it's worth making your way up to **Hautvillers**. Although a little bit touristy and self-conscious, this picturesque old village has glorious views and has reason to be proud of its past. For it was in the abbey here in the 17th century that the monk Dom Perignon, eager to give the local wine a sparkle, devised the *méthode champenoise*. Champagne has been famous ever since. Dom Perignon is buried in the former abbey church, now Hautvillers' parish church.

South of Épernay ·rises the CÔTES DES BLANCS, hillsides covered with the white Chardonnay grapevine. Although all champagne is white (unless coloured pink with a splash of red wine), it is made largely with red grapes. Only 25 per cent of the blend is white grapes, and these all come from the Côte des Blancs. Just a few champagnes, called *blanc des blancs*, are made only of white grapes. They are subtler and more elegant. At the summit of the slope there are extensive areas of forest. From the wine village of **Pierry**, D10 and D9 pass through other distinguished champagne villages – **Cuis**, **Cramant** (noted for a less foaming variety of champagne), **Avize**, **Oger** – as far as **Vertus**, with its natural springs and 11th-century church.

TARDENOIS AND BRIE

30 km–70 km from Reims

This western fringe of the old county of Champagne is over the départemental border in the Aisne, and is untypical of the rest of the Champagne region. The landscape is quite different, being higher, hillier and devoted to pastoral rather than arable farming. There are muddy farms and homely, rustic green fields with contented cows instead of the clean lines, unbroken horizons and broad swaths of colour more familiar in the rest of the farming country of Champagne.

Both Tardenois and Brie extend out of Champagne towards Paris. Brie is famous for its cheese, but the best of it comes from the farms around Meaux, beyond the limits of Champagne. This is also a region of castles, now all ruined, which serve as a reminder that Champagne has seen its difficult periods in history.

Just outside **Fère-en-Tardenois** (*50 km from Reims*), striking castle ruins are combined with one of the Champagne country's best hotel-restaurants. The castle at Fère, originally built in the early 13th century as a defensive royal fortress, was given in

1528 as a wedding present to the immensely powerful Connétable de France, Anne de Montmorency (who was very much a man, despite the name). He transformed it into a country residence and had a fine Renaissance gallery built across the deep moat. The castle eventually came into the hands of post-Revolutionary monarch Philippe Égalité who largely destroyed and defaced it to win popularity. In 1863 the surviving later section of the château, standing outside the moat, was fully restored. This building became, in 1956, the present-day **Hostellerie du Château** (tel. 23.82.21.13), a superb hotel of style, with a famous restaurant. It's by no means inexpensive, but is a wonderful place for a celebration weekend.

The little town of Fère itself is an agreeable local centre, with an interesting 16th-century open-sided covered market.

Château-Thierry (*55 km from Reims*), rising from the broad river Marne, retains the outer walls of another famous hilltop castle. However, despite a few old houses, this is not a particularly attractive town. The site of the château is now essentially a public park, from which a wide view of the surrounding country is ruined by the sight of a huge ugly factory. In the countryside on the other side of the Marne there's a better-preserved 16th-century château (originally 12th century) at the village of **Condé-en-Brie** (*50 km from Reims*) beside the river Dhuys. A few kilometres south, **Montmirail** also has a good 16th-century château in Louis XIII style. Just outside this quiet little country town, once fortified, on 11 February 1814 Napoleon took on the combined armies of Russia and Prussia – and beat them soundly.

L'ÉPINE AND CHÂLONS-SUR-MARNE

45 km–52 km from Reims

Once one of the great trading cities of old Champagne, ancient **Châlons-sur-Marne** was the victim of much wartime damage in this century. Rebuilt, it survives as a large characterless industrial town with some tasteless modern architecture. At its old centre, not far from the river, there's a rather neglected Gothic cathedral with worn and blackened stonework. However, it has interesting twin spires and some good stone-carving. There are several other notable churches in town, the most impressive being Notre-Dame-en-Vaux, which dates mainly from the 12th century. It has distinctive spires and attractive cloisters. Châlons has always been a centre for cloth manufacture and of the champagne wine trade, and now also has many other industries, including brewing.

Another remarkable church can be seen some 7 km to the east at **L'Épine**, an appealing little village where flower beds decorate the street. The pale, beautiful Gothic basilica of Notre Dame de l'Épine has some resemblance to Reims Cathedral. Dating from the early 16th century, it has an elaborately carved exterior, with two handsome galleried towers of openwork carving. Inside, the building is light and lofty, and was gloriously filled with organ music on the day I visited.

Apart from its basilica, L'Épine boasts another great institution, the hotel-restaurant **Aux Armes de Champagne** (tel. 26.66.96.79). This is renowned as one of the best places to eat in the whole Champagne region. The premises are not especially grand, but the restaurant is stylish and civilized. The hotel occupies several fairly modest buildings, with comfortable but very varied rooms. Ask to face on to the garden rather than the street. Prices both for accommodation and in the dining room are on the high side. Nevertheless, ease of access (via autoroute A26 and then from Châlons), the village setting beside the basilica and the superb food make this a tempting Champagne base at any price.

TROYES

122 km from Reims

Although in the far south of the Champagne country, and at a considerable distance from the vineyards and other places of interest, this former capital of the Counts of Champagne should not be disregarded. The city centre is in two sections, one of

which, the eastern half, is bounded by the river Seine, the other
– the older, western part of town – by boulevards and gardens
which replaced the medieval ramparts. Between the two runs the
Canal de la Haute Seine, partly covered by roads. In both halves
of town, but especially at the heart of the western district, is a
large central area of picturesque old half-timbered dwellings.
Most of these historic buildings have been beautifully restored.

A simple way to see what the city has to offer is to take the
Rue de la Cité, the narrow old through-road, from one end to
the other. It starts at the Gothic and Renaissance church of
St Nizier, which has a handsome Burgundian-style patterned tile
roof. Within a few metres the road reaches the cathedral, a large
edifice in pale stone, its west front an overwhelming mass of
swirling, Flamboyant design. The interior, dating from an earlier
phase of Gothic, is more restrained and elegant, and possesses a
surprising amount of superb stained glass. Particularly striking
is the impressive 16th-century rose window in the transept.
Beside the cathedral, in the former Archbishop's Palace, there's
a first-class museum of modern art. Concentrating mainly on
French Post-Impressionist painting, it has a remarkable collection of Fauves. The contents of the whole museum were a gift
to the town in 1976 from prominent local businessman Pierre
Levy.

Continue on the same street, which changes its name to Rue
Clemenceau, across a canal into the western half of town. Just
across the water is the church of St Urbain, of interest to
architecture enthusiasts for its unusual early-Gothic interior.
The road enters Place Maréchal Foch, the big main square at the
centre of Troyes. West and south of it, and around the church of
St Jean, are some really delightful medieval streets and little
squares, well preserved and traffic-free, lined with charming
overhanging half-timbered buildings. Their ground floors are
now, with few exceptions, converted into small shops. It is
enjoyable to stroll here, taking a break as necessary at the
tempting bars and restaurants.

Explore a little more and you will discover in this old quarter
of Troyes several distinguished *hôtels*, grand town houses, some
dating to the 16th and 17th centuries. One of them, Hôtel de

Troyes

Vauluisant in Rue de Vauluisant, a lovely 16th-century house with turrets and traditional chequerboard façade, contains an interesting Musée Historique (Historical Museum). Part of the museum traces the history of Troyes through the centuries, with old maps and prints; and there's an unusual painting of Jews in 16th-century Troyes, which as a major trading town has always had a large Jewish population. In the 11th century there was an important Talmudic school here. There's a sizeable, but discreet, synagogue located in half-timbered premises in the city centre just off Rue Salengro.

Troyes has several other museums and churches of note. Among the most interesting museums is the Musée de l'Outil et de la Pensée Ouvrière (Museum of Implements and Workers' Thought). This unusual museum, with fascinating displays of the hand tools used in Troyes's traditional crafts (including *bonneterie*, hat-making, for which the city was long famous), as well as a library, is housed in a superb 16th-century mansion in Rue de la Trinité.

4. UPPER NORMANDY

Seine Maritime and Eure

Getting there

There are two ferry ports in Upper Normandy: Dieppe and Le Havre. Dieppe is the smaller and by far the more pleasant town, but Le Havre has better road connections. Most of Upper Normandy is not appreciably closer to one port than the other.

Dieppe is 4 hours from Newhaven on Sealink, with usually about four crossings daily (fewer in winter). Le Havre is 5¾ hours from Portsmouth (longer at night) on P&O, with usually three crossings daily.

NORMANDY's two eastern départements make a sharp contrast to the rest of the province. While Normandy as a whole feels profoundly rustic and old-fashioned, with small farms and abundant woods and copses, here the landscape opens out under broad, bright skies and presents a picture of wide fields, almost treeless horizons and large-scale agriculture.

Upper Normandy divides naturally into three regions, of which the largest extends from the river Seine north-east nearly to the borders of Picardy. This is the Pays de Caux, a productive chalk plain of stark lines which reaches the sea in high dazzling white cliffs. The strong point here is the impressive coast and its charming resort towns. Next in size is the area south of the Seine, where the land is almost as flat and open, though more varied, with more to catch the eye, and scattered with a few towns and villages of interest. Finally, on the northern and eastern margins of the Caux, there are the magnificent beech forests – Lyons, Eawy, Arques and smaller woodlands – and the big patch of picturesque greenery known as the Pays de Bray. This is a pleasant country of apple orchards and, above all, dairy farms.

Through all of this flows the mighty Seine, coiled and twisting like a serpent, a river of character and history which captures the essence of Upper Normandy. Navigable (with difficulty) all the

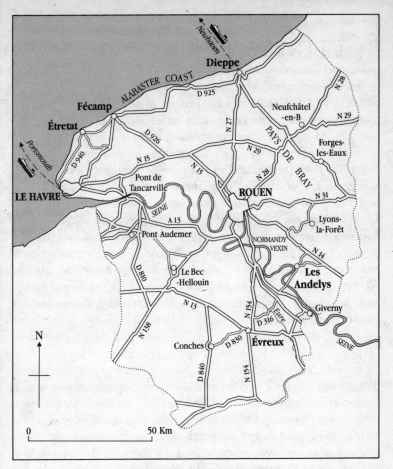

UPPER NORMANDY

way into Paris, the Seine has been through long centuries a major highway. For the Vikings, or Normans as they were called here, the rich towns and monasteries of the Seine were an open invitation. When the Normans gave up the plundering life, their meeting in the year 911 with the Frankish king Charles the Simple took place at St Clair on the Epte, a tributary of the Seine. The Epte became the boundary of a new Duchy of

Normandy, everything to its west being ceded to the former raiders.

Since they themselves had been the only threat menacing the peace and prosperity of the land, and as they were able defenders of their new home, the Normans were able to create a well-ordered and civilized society. For them too the Seine was the most important highway, its tributaries like side roads into the interior. Monasteries and towns along the riverbanks were re-built in a 'Norman' style that was carried into all their colonies – from England and Ireland to the eastern Mediterranean. Indeed, the Normans of Upper Normandy were the most adventurous and skilful of the province's exploring seamen. There's even a Little Dieppe on the coast of Guinea, founded in 1364; a team of Protestant seamen from Le Havre established a colony on the Brazilian coast in 1555; while Cavalier de la Salle, whose name is still proudly recalled in Québec, sailed from Rouen across the Atlantic, through the St Lawrence seaway to the Great Lakes and down the Mississippi, eventually claiming Louisiana for France in 1682.

À table

The hearty appetite and love of rich, high-quality foods which characterize the rest of Normandy are just as much in evidence here. Most towns and villages of Upper Normandy stand beside water, so tradition has dictated that in this region fish and seafood play an even greater part in the diet. Le Havre and Rouen are both great ports, but from scores of much smaller fishing harbours too the fresh catch is quickly dispatched to the kitchens of the region's homes and restaurants. Fécamp and Dieppe on the coast have famous daily fresh fish markets. At Dieppe's wonderful and extensive street market you'll discover oysters, clams, scallops and mussels loaded high on the tempting stalls. Sole (*sole*), brill (*barbue*) and mackerel (*maquereau*) are seen with almost monotonous frequency on the menus of Upper Normandy, served with the usual luscious cider-and-cream *sauce Normande* – here made with fish stock. Dieppe has given its name to several of Upper Normandy's specialities. *Marmite*

Dieppoise is a herb-flavoured stew of fish and shellfish. *Sole à la Dieppoise* has the fish cooked in cider (or, less correctly, wine) with shallots, and the sauce thickened with cream and butter.

Among the meats, tripe sausages, black pudding and pâtés from Caen, Vire and the Perche (all in the next-door départements of Calvados and Orne) are just as popular here. One gruesome local speciality is the Rouen duckling, *caneton Rouennais*, which is killed by suffocation to keep in the blood. The blood is then squeezed out and mixed with cream to make a sauce. Perhaps you'd prefer to stick to fish!

Crème fraîche, that incomparable thick tangy speciality of Normandy, is generously used, and the great Norman farmhouse cheeses of the Pays d'Auge – Camembert, Livarot and Pont l'Évêque – don't have far to come. Upper Normandy produces distinctive soft and white creamy cheeses of its own in the Pays de Bray. The best known is ultra-mild, factory-made Petit-Suisse, which is a relatively recent invention, but there's also triple-cream Brillat-Savarin, which is even more recent, as well as traditional, distinguished Neufchâtel, which can be either mild and fresh or strong and aged. Explore the markets and you will find other fresh cheeses from the farms of Bray.

Bray makes cider as well as cheese. In any case the apple orchards of the Pays d'Auge are not far away, so as in the rest of Normandy dry cider is the traditional drink with food, while sparkling *pommeau* (made of cider with Calvados) makes a good aperitif, and a double of Calvados, Normandy's powerful but elegant apple spirit, completes a good dinner.

DIEPPE

Ferry port, 104 km from Le Havre

Probably no other Channel port gives disembarking ferry passengers such an immediate and satisfying impression of stepping ashore straight into the heart of France. Because of the length of the sea crossing, and the lack of useful autoroute connections, Dieppe is not nowadays among the most popular arrival points.

As a result, this handsome town escapes being overrun by the boorish beery Brits so common in some other Channel ports. It's an important local centre for the whole Caux region, and is, besides, one of Normandy's main fishing harbours, so it's crowded instead with French shoppers.

In the last century Dieppe was a favourite resort of the well-to-do British. If a line were drawn straight from London to Paris, as often used to be said, Dieppe would be almost exactly halfway along it. The town lacked the slightly disreputable quality which attached to Boulogne, yet was acceptably raffish. Here too, people who found it socially difficult to live in Britain often placed themselves in pleasant voluntary exile. The town, with its glorious skies and open sea views, also attracted the Impressionists. Many a famous painting chose as its subject the colour and light of the Dieppe waterfront.

Despite a long history of tourism, fish and fishing are still the *raison d'être* of the town. Although Dieppe appears to be situated on a long sandy beach, the sea carves a deep natural harbour into the land at this point. The town's name is an almost unaltered Norse word, Dyepp, which means 'deep'. The old town – although the port itself had to be largely rebuilt after the war – clusters around this inland harbour, and this is where Channel ferries dock. The beach therefore lies 'behind' the town, and the two aspects of Dieppe – sedate resort and hard-working port – are slightly separate, the one facing out to sea, the other looking in to the ancient quaysides.

Although there has been some rebuilding, the old quarter has tremendous charm and atmosphere. Ships and small boats in the port are right in the middle of town. On the quays fish are bought and sold, and cooked in many excellent little restaurants. Early in the morning, the watersides are alive with stalls selling the fresh catch of turbot, sole, brill and shellfish. Over half the *coquilles St Jacques* (scallops) eaten in France come from here. On the far side of the harbour you can see the picturesque Le Pollet district where most of the fishing families live. On handsome Quai Henri IV, where the ferries arrive, there are three excellent fish restaurants perfect for sampling traditional

Dieppoise cooking at its best for very modest prices: **Armorique,
La Musardière** and **Le Port**.

Within a few paces of the docks, Grande Rue is the pedestrianized main street. It's a joy of fine little food shops, stores with
smart clothes and best-quality kitchenware, and a contented
civilized bustle. Opening on to its left, Place Nationale is the
centre of the big Saturday market which spills along Grande
Rue. This has been an eye-opener for many a British tourist,
accustomed to the lifeless pasteurized products of Britain's Milk
Marketing Board, discovering here for the first time just what
cream, butter and cheese were intended to be. Even the experi-
enced francophile will be impressed by the range and quality of
farm-made produce on the stalls here. At the end of Place
Nationale looms Dieppe's large St Jacques church in a mixture
of styles from 12th-century Romanesque to Flamboyant Gothic
to Renaissance.

Jehan Ango is buried inside. A lawless 16th-century pirate,
Ango is the ancestor of whom the Dieppois are most proud.
Shops, hotels and restaurants are named after him. As a 'privateer' loyal to his king, Ango robbed and captured hundreds of
foreign vessels. He virtually destroyed the whole Portuguese
merchant fleet, an act regarded as tremendously laudable and
patriotic by the French of that period.

Grande Rue ends at Place du Puit Salé, a focal square with
several popular café-bars. Among them is the **Café des Tribunaux**, an 18th-century auberge of great character. Its dingy interior was the place Oscar Wilde preferred for a drink during his
sad exile here during the 1890s after his release from Reading
Gaol. The wasted figure of Aubrey Beardsley would also have
been seen here at the same time. A decade before them the
Tribunaux had been patronized by a livelier crowd of young
artists of the new Impressionist movement, including many
destined to become world famous: Renoir, Monet, Pissarro,
Sickert and Whistler.

Round the corner in Rue St Jacques there are more excellent
shops. There's a wonderful cheese shop here, Épicier Olivier. It
was set up by Claude Olivier, father of Philippe Olivier who runs
the famous cheese shop in Boulogne.

If, for speed and convenience, you prefer to shop at a hyper-market, head out to the Mammouth Centre Commercial on the Rouen road.

The beach side of town consists of a string of hotels, mostly only of a modest standard but some still preserving a *fin-de-siècle* style, along Boulevard de Verdun. Between the boulevard and the sea is a broad, attractive grass-covered esplanade. Below the greensward there's a pebbly beach. On fine days, in summer, it's sheer delight to walk on this wide green space full of light and air. The boulevard ends at the Château, which dates from the 15th century (it can be reached directly from the town centre by continuing from Grande Rue along Rue de la Barre, and climbing the steps of Rue de Chastes). It now houses a museum which has a mainly nautical theme, although there is also an interesting collection of carved ivories made in Dieppe during the Middle Ages, and there are several good Impressionist works.

LE HAVRE

Ferry port, 104 km from Dieppe

Perhaps the least appealing of the French Channel ports, with its vast industrial districts exuding poisonous fumes, this is decidedly a place to get away from rather than go to. The town centre is all straight lines of post-war concrete. Of course, it's not Le Havre's fault that it was totally destroyed in 1944 and had to be quickly rebuilt. Nor is it really Le Havre's fault that the architect who recreated the town (Auguste Perret) was one of the fathers of that prevailing school of modern architects who believe that concrete is a suitable material for buildings. Admittedly, Perret's concrete Le Havre is something grander than mere utilitarianism; there are fine broad boulevards and well-planned spaces of greenery and flowers.

In any case, the place does have *some* attractions. It's a great town for shopping. The main street, Avenue Foch, has stores as chic as in Paris. It ends at the immense Place de l'Hôtel de Ville. Rue de Paris, leading south out of the Place, is another smart shopping street, as is Avenue Réné Coty, north of the square. In Avenue Coty there's a street market every Monday, Wednesday and Friday. If you prefer hypermarket shopping, the vast Auchan can be found in the suburb Mont-Gaillard about ten minutes' drive from the city centre. Worth a visit is the exceptional Musée des Beaux-Arts André Malraux (André Malraux Museum of Fine Arts), a glass-and-steel structure containing a good collection of Impressionists and Post-Impressionists. The museum is close to the ferry terminal, at the meeting point of Boulevard Clemenceau and Chaussée John Kennedy.

Along the main streets you'll have ample choice of bars at which to relax over a coffee and watch the world go by. If it's lunch or dinner time, consider a meal in the art-nouveau surroundings of **Lescalle** (tel. 35.43.07.93), on a corner in the Place de l'Hôtel de Ville. This was Jean-Paul Sartre's favourite restaurant when he lived in the town, but presumably it was cheaper and more down to earth in those days. Hotels and restaurants are numerous, nearly all being within about 300 metres of the sea. The very nicest part of Le Havre is **Ste Adresse**, a pleasant suburb with excellent views over the sea and port: here too there are some small, welcoming hotels. But Le Havre's greatest advantage is its ease of access to some of the most interesting and enjoyable parts of Normandy. To the south lies the Pays d'Auge (see Chapter 5), east is the Seine valley, and north the dignified white-cliffed coast of the Pays de Caux.

ALABASTER COAST

From Dieppe to Étretat, total about 80 km

Upper Normandy's Pays de Caux meets the sea in immensely high white cliffs of chalk layered with flint. The cliffs are sculpted and broken by occasional river estuaries around which cluster agreeable resorts. Some of these were once very smart, which did not stop them having thriving fishing fleets, while some of the smaller towns and villages along the shore were never resorts at all but remained simple fishing communities until the present day. It is impressive and exhilarating to walk on the broad sands beside the towering cliffs under a vast sky – everything on this coast seems on a huge scale. The chalky paleness of the rock has given it the name Côte d'Albâtre, the Alabaster Coast. A succession of minor roads connect to form a village-to-village drive just inland from this peaceful, scenic coast.

Varengeville-sur-Mer (*8 km from Dieppe*) is picturesque, and fascinated the Impressionists. The stained glass in the church was designed by painter Georges Braque, who is buried in the cemetery. Just ½ km away up a lovely avenue of beeches is the manor house which was built by Dieppe's 16th-century privateer Jehan Ango. Its most striking feature is the remarkable dovecote in the central courtyard. Little **Ste-Marguerite** (*12 km from Dieppe*) and, just off the coast road, **Bourg-Dun** both have interesting old churches. At pretty **Veules-les-Roses** (*24 km from Dieppe*) there's an excellent restaurant, **Les Galets** (3 Rue Victor Hugo, tel. 35.97.61.33). **St Valéry-en-Caux** (*34 km from Dieppe*) is a thriving little fishing port, overlooked by a large comfortable modern hotel, the **Altea** (14 Avenue Clemenceau, tel. 35.97.35.48). It perhaps spoils the view, but you may find it a useful place to stay. From **Veulettes-sur-Mer** (*41 km from Dieppe*) for some 20 km, the road is especially pleasing and attractive.

Fécamp (*72 km from Dieppe, 30 km from Le Havre*) is a busy, industrial port enclosed by the cliffs. The harbour is the focal point of this congenial town, which provides the background to several novels written by Guy de Maupassant. He was born on the quay (at no. 82), which has been renamed after him. There's a good market on Saturdays. It's an old place, originally a Gallic and then a Roman settlement. It was first put on the map when thousands of exceedingly gullible pilgrims flocked here to see a lead casket containing 'drops of the Holy Blood' which had been washed ashore in the hollowed-out trunk of what was supposed to be a fig tree. A monastery was founded here in AD 633 to protect this 'precious blood', as it became known. In the 11th century Richard II of England built the lovely church of La Trinité to house the dubious relic, and he re-established the monastery as a glorious Benedictine abbey in the style of Cluny, where he had just been. The abbey grew immensely wealthy – the Bishop of Dol (in Brittany) waxed lyrical about the plethora of 'gold, silver and silken ornaments' – and for centuries great numbers of pilgrims journeyed to the church, especially at Easter.

While the blood story is not to everyone's taste, in the 16th century the Benedictines at Fécamp created a more palatable elixir, their liqueur, Bénédictine, distilled from plants growing on the cliffs. The distillery, inside an extraordinary, palatial 19th-century mock-Gothic edifice, has become the main business of the abbey. It can be visited (March to November) on guided tours which reveal the fragrant ingredients but not the formula for the precious brew, and there is a museum devoted to the history of the liqueur.

Richard's original Trinité church was destroyed by fire, and rebuilt in 1175 in the early Gothic style, but has been much altered and added to over the centuries. The result is not altogether pleasing despite some beautiful elements within the building. It is still much frequented by credulous pilgrims. Richard I and Richard II of England are both buried here.

Étretat (*90 km from Dieppe, 17 km from Le Havre*) is a summer-only resort. In the high season it's popular and convivial, visited by many French families, even though the beach is pebbly. It offers all the usual delights, including a notable golf course, but these amenities are open only for two or three months in the year. The town's great asset, in any season, is the green-topped white cliffs rising to either side, which have been hewn into bizarre shapes by the waves and weather. Most conspicuous are two weird natural arches, one each end of the beach. All this can be amply appreciated from the clifftop walks, which give glorious views up the white-fringed coast. In town there's an 11th- and 12th-century Romanesque church, delightful in spite of some unfortunate 19th-century alterations. Many artists and writers have especially liked modest little Étretat, and several bought houses here. Victor Hugo, Guy de Maupassant and Gustav Flaubert all declared their love for this seaside town, and

Curious cliff formations at Etretat

a steady stream of Impressionists came here to paint. There are many middle-priced, middle-quality hotels. Most tempting of them is the **Dormy House** on the Le Havre road (tel. 35.27.07. 88), a quiet place with excellent views of the Alabaster Coast.

PAYS DE BRAY

20 km–75 km from Dieppe

The Bray region is one of the prettiest parts of Upper Normandy, a land of greenery, dairy farms and orchards. It's noted for many variations of soft white creamy cheese. You'll come across them in shops and markets in all the towns of the area. Around the edges of the Pays de Bray are some beautiful forests perfect for touring by car or, better still, on foot.

The best-known of Bray cheeses is Neufchâtel. Smooth and tangy, it's mild but creamy when fresh, strong and salty when ripened, and is made into a choice of different shapes, each with its own name. The most traditional local shape is a short cylindrical roll, called bondon. Confusingly though, there's an-

other Bray farmhouse cheese called bondon – or bondard or
bonde – which is the same shape; it's a fresh white cheese
ripened for anything from a couple of days to a couple of
months, the flavour intensifying considerably with the passage
of time. Demi-sel is another soft, smooth, white Bray cheese, but
factory-made with pasteurized milk. Petit-Suisse, also made here,
is similar but unsalted, mild and watery. A very high-fat version,
but tasting more like butter than cheese, is Brillat-Savarin.

Neufchâtel-en-Bray (*36 km from Dieppe, 45 km from Rouen*) is
the capital of the Pays de Bray, and is the centre of the trade in
Neufchâtel and other Bray cheeses. As a result of wartime
destruction, it's an unprepossessing place. It has a good market,
though, on Tuesday and Saturday mornings, and makes a possible base for trips into the glorious **Forêt d'Eawy**. This extensive
area of mature beech woods covers a rocky ridge of land
reaching from a point 10 km west of Neufchâtel over halfway to
Dieppe. Under its leafy branches there are several agreeable
drives and paths, including the straight Allée des Limousins
which cuts right through, crossing deep wooded valleys. The
name, by the way, is pronounced Ee-aa-vee. In the other direction, 10 km north of Neufchâtel, the **Basse Forêt d'Eu** is
similar though on a much smaller scale. Another 5 km further
north, you reach the edges of the **Haute Forêt d'Eu**, between
the two in size and again covering high ground. On the far side,
the Eu forest descends to the river Bresle, the border with
Picardy.

Forges-les-Eaux (*50 km from Dieppe, 42 km from Rouen*), in
the midst of the loveliest part of the Bray country, gets the
'forges' part of its name from the days when this was a centre of
industry and ironwork. But that was 500 years ago, and now it's
the 'eaux' which predominates. Forges is a most appealing little
spa resort, with an elegant park where you can taste 'the waters',
and one or two attractive old buildings. The Forge's spring water
is drunk to cure anaemia among other things, and it was
believed to be this condition that made Anne of Austria, wife of
Louis XIII, unable to have a baby. The efficacy of the spa may
perhaps be judged from the fact that although Anne and Louis
came to drink from the curative springs in 1632, it was not until

1639 that their baby was born. The town is the centre for the marketing of Brillat-Savarin cheese, and there are some modest small hotels with good restaurants.

Gournay-en-Bray (*70 km from Dieppe, 50 km from Rouen*), with the river Epte frontier running right through town, is half in Normandy and half in Picardy. It is the main centre for the manufacture of Petit-Suisse cheeses. The town is unremarkable, but it has an interesting old church, and benefits from being right on the fringes on the lovely **Forêt de Lyons**. The forest is a big, satisfying area of beech woods, peaceful hamlets, ruined castles and abbeys, and wonderful walks. Once it was all a hunting preserve of the Dukes of Normandy.

At the heart of the forest, the small picturesque town of **Lyons-la-Forêt** (*65 km from Dieppe on back-roads, 35 km from Rouen*), with its old flower-decked wooden houses and market-place, is supremely attractive and pleasing – out of season. In summer, inevitably such a gorgeous place is overrun by tourists. Henry I of England died in Lyons-la-Forêt after that 'surfeit of lampreys' which has gone down in history. He had eaten the previous night at the Cistercians' now-ruined Mortemer Abbey, 4 km away (today it contains a museum of monastic life). Fortunately I did not see lampreys (eels) on the menu at the **Le Grand Cerf** (Place du Marché, tel. 32.49.60.44), an excellent hotel-restaurant with traditional Normandy fish dishes (pricey), a handful of pretty rooms (reasonable) and a view of the market.

ROUEN

61 km from Dieppe, 90 km from Le Havre

A curve in the wildly twisting Seine pushes itself right into the centre of Rouen, Normandy's historic capital and a great river port. The site was ideal for an important town, at this very first (or last) place on the Seine where a bridge could be constructed, which happened also to be exceptionally well protected by hills, yet approachable by valleys. The Romans realized its potential and built the first Rouen, which they called Rotomagus. It has been a major port ever since.

During their 1940 invasion, the Germans destroyed a great deal of the city; and to drive the Germans out, the 1944 liberation caused yet more damage. Today's rebuilt Rouen is frankly ugly, with its miles of industry, concrete and modern 'architecture'. Yet though most of post-war Rouen is large and unsightly, the old quarter at its centre, with its spires and belfries rising above the roofs, is picturesque and walkable. It was once bounded by mighty walls, but where these once stood there now runs a busy inner ring road of boulevards.

Mercifully, most of the old heart of Rouen was able to be repaired and restored after the wartime onslaughts, and it is a delight to wander in its narrow old lanes. Be warned: as soon as the tourist year starts at Easter, and until it ends in October, there are plenty of visitors here; the best time to come is well out of season, perhaps in the first warm rays of spring sunshine.

A good starting point for a walk through the old town is Place du Vieux-Marché (with underground parking), at one end of old Rouen's main street Rue du Gros-Horloge. An event of great significance took place in this square in 1431. Towards the end of the Hundred Years War, the French were exhausted while the English were on the brink of victory. Had they won, France and England would have become a single kingdom under a monarch of Norman descent. In 1420, by a treaty signed at Troyes, Henry V of England was already recognized as King of France. At this point the mysterious Jeanne d'Arc appeared on the scene. In effect a madwoman hearing voices, driven by burning inner flames of religion and patriotism, she dressed as a man and dramatically turned the fortunes of the French. She led them in victory against the English at Orléans, urged the heir to the French throne to come out of hiding and be crowned at Reims, and was eventually captured at Compiègne by the Burgundians (allies of the English). They handed her over to the English at Rouen, where she was tried – not by Englishmen but by a French ecclesiastical court, on a charge of heresy – and finally burnt alive on 30 May 1431 in Rouen's Place du Vieux-Marché.

The exact spot is marked by a grim 65 foot concrete cross in the square. Far from giving advantage to the English, the burning of Joan of Arc caused a huge upsurge of resistance among the French. With amazing rapidity the English were defeated and driven out of France. At the same time, the Duchy of Normandy was abolished, in 1469, to become instead a province of the French crown. Yet only as recently as 1920 was Joan of Arc made a Catholic saint and declared patron saint of France.

As the name of the Place suggests, this was the market-place of pre-war Rouen, and thanks to several attractive half-timbered 17th- and 18th-century dwellings it's easy to imagine how it once looked. There's a museum of Joan of Arc in one of the houses. The rebuilt Place has been split into two, with a new covered market-place in one section, and the tall Joan of Arc memorial cross in the other, together with a weird-looking modern church – containing some excellent 16th-century stained glass, however – dedicated to St Joan.

From the Place the next step must be to wander up Rue du Gros-Horloge, the main street through the old quarter. It's free of traffic, lined with lovely timbered 14th-century buildings, and must have featured in a hundred thousand tourist snapshots. This is also a real shopping street busy with locals. Its name comes from the town's most characteristic landmark, the Gros Horloge, an ornate Renaissance tower with a large blue, gold and red clock face on each side, spanning the street. It dates from 1527. The taller domed belfry beside it is some two or three centuries older, and still rings the ancient curfew bell at nine o'clock every night. You can go inside, up the 16th-century spiral stairs, and from the top get a superb view across the old town.

Rue du Gros-Horloge ends in Place de la Cathédrale, facing one of the finest Gothic buildings in Europe. The square itself has many medieval and Renaissance buildings; one of them, House of the Exchequer (opposite the cathedral), is occupied by Rouen's tourist office. Notre-Dame Cathedral was started in 1145 but not finished until 1514 – although there were later alterations, including the addition of the distinctive metal spire

Le Gros Horloge at Rouen

in the 19th century. Repairs of wartime damage are still continuing. The building is fascinating for its harmonious diversity and its well-conceived intricacy of decorative Gothic stonework. The exquisite lace-like tracery of the 16th-century west front is framed by the relative simplicity of the early Gothic Tour St Romain on one side and, on the other, the exuberant flamboyance of the late Gothic Tour de Beurre (Butter Tower, paid for by rich citizens in exchange for the right to eat butter during Lent – how's that for piety?). The Impressionist painter Monet, fascinated more by light than by architecture, placed his easel in the Place de la Cathédrale and painted the complex façade of Notre-Dame twenty times as the sunlight struck the stonework at different hours of the day.

Take a leisurely look at the exterior from all sides. The south face has a superb 14th-century doorway called Portail de la

Calende, while on the north side the Portail des Libraires (Book-sellers' Doorway, given its name on account of the bookstalls which used to cluster on this side of the cathedral) is arguably even more beautiful. Inside, there's more superb stone-carving and marvellous stained-glass windows old and new. The tombs in the cathedral show the importance of Rouen since the days of the first Normans. The Viking warrior Rollo, first Duke of Normandy, is buried here. Around him lie many nobles of the great Anglo-Norman dynasty he founded. It was Rollo who, having been granted Rouen as capital of his new duchy, deepened the shipping canal, drained the surrounding marshland and constructed sturdy quays which lasted 1,000 years.

Stepping out of the cathedral, turn right and right again into narrow Rue St Romain, which, like many others, is lined with magnificent half-timbered dwellings of the 15th to 18th centuries. The street ends at Rue de la République. Cross over this main road to reach another impressive and unusual Flamboyant Gothic church, St Maclou. The façade is bow-shaped, and the doorways highly decorated; two of the doors have exquisitely carved Renaissance panels. Inside there's more excellent 16th-century wood-carving, especially the spiral stairs and organ loft. The 'cloister' in Rue Martainville just north-east, called Aître St Maclou, is a courtyard of early 16th-century half-timbered build-ings and was in fact a former plague cemetery; its wooden galleries have fascinating carvings on the theme of death.

Go back to the front of St Maclou and turn into Rue Damiette, another street of superb old half-timbered houses. It leads to-wards the tall octagonal lantern tower soaring above the third of Rouen's three great Gothic churches, St Ouen. This former abbey church, larger than the cathedral, was built during the 14th and 15th centuries while the Hundred Years War raged all around. It achieved a cool, unemotional architectural perfection. The interior proportions are in perfect equilibrium, there's good stonework and wood-carving, as well as some fine 14th-century stained glass, and the organ is one of the largest in France. You can hear it during the annual season of summer concerts.

Rouen has many museums. A couple well worth seeing are within a short walk of St Ouen church, and if you have been to the belfry in Rue du Gros-Horloge your entrance ticket will also permit entry to these two museums. To reach them, walk along Rue de l'Hôpital and Rue Ganterie and you will pass a Gothic fountain and some attractive old houses. Turn right into Rue de l'Écureuil, and it's a few paces to one of Rouen's busiest streets, Rue Thiers. On the other side of the road stand the Musée Le Secq de Tournelles, inside a former Gothic church, and, much larger, the Musée des Beaux-Arts (Fine Arts Museum). The former has interesting displays of ironwork dating from the 3rd century to the 19th. The latter has exceptional collections of traditional Rouen ceramics and pottery, and an impressive selection of European paintings up to the present day. The highlights are Flemish works of the 16th and 17th centuries, and leading Impressionists Monet and Sisley.

There's much more to see in town, including the quaysides of the port, several fine churches, half a dozen more museums and plenty of delightful streets with houses several centuries old. If you want somewhere to sit and linger over a coffee or drink, or maybe even a simple meal, there are several good bars and brasseries in and around Place du Vieux-Marché. For a proper lunch or dinner the same area offers a wide choice of decent restaurants, and there are others scattered around the old quarter. One worth noting: the legendary **Bertrand Warin** (7–9 Rue de la Pie, tel. 35.89.26.69), just off Place du Vieux Marché, is delightful with its courtyard, and has glorious food at fairly high prices. In between the bars and restaurants of Place du Vieux-Marché, there are superb food shops.

Places to stay are not so easy to find. There are several modern budget hotels or motels on the outskirts of the city, but this is very poor alternative to staying close to the old quarter. **Hôtel Dieppe** (Place B. Tissot, tel. 35.71.96.00), outside the old quarter, and close to the railway station, is comfortable and has a good restaurant serving traditional dishes of Upper Normandy. **Colin's Hotel** (15 Rue Pie, tel. 35.71.00.88) is a modern place just off the Place, and though not cheap is good value for such a central location. Alternatively, stay well out of town – say, at Les Andelys or at La Bouille – and visit Rouen for the day.

LOWER SEINE VALLEY

From Le Havre to Rouen: 90 km

From Le Havre to Rouen as the crow flies is hardly more than 60 km. But only a crow can travel that way up the serpentine Seine valley between the two cities. The Seine's current is brisk, but for all that the course of the river is coiled and meandering to the extent that sometimes places on the banks which are some 15 km apart by water are barely a couple of kilometres away from one another by land. Much of the distance from Le Havre to Rouen is through rich handsome woodland. To either side are the remains of old abbeys and castles, reminders of the days when this stretch of river was the busiest thoroughfare in the Duchy of Normandy.

The first stage of the journey upriver runs along an autoroute from Le Havre to Tancarville beside the Seine's huge estuary. The scene is horribly disfigured by the necessities of industry, mainly oil refining and the manufacture of petrochemical derivatives. Wind up the windows and press on. On the far side of the bay, Honfleur (see Chapter 5) can just be seen. For most travellers the name **Tancarville** (*28 km from Le Havre*) means only a long high toll-bridge over the Seine. This in itself is a sight worth seeing, and it is remarkable that until 1959 there was no bridge at all over the Seine between Le Havre and Rouen, although there were and are many places where it can be crossed by ferry (a slow process, and suitable only for light vehicles). Beside the bridge, though, there is an old village with a ruined castle built by Henry I of England. Only the so-called Eagle Tower survives intact. Standing on a rocky spur, it has a commanding view of the estuary. Up the road at **Lillebonne** (*37 km from Le Havre*), the Gauls' capital of the Caux region, there are ruins of a grander castle originally built for William the Conqueror.

Crossing the lofty Tancarville bridge, the road skirts a curious area of cultivated drained marshland, the Marais Vernier, which until the mid-19th century was submerged beneath the waters of the river Seine. On the far side of the marshland the road climbs out of the Seine valley to reach **Pont Audemer** on the river Risle. Although its outer ring is less than appealing, the centre of this ancient town is exceptionally picturesque. Timbered houses, some with wrought-iron balconies, hang over narrow streets and waterways that thread through the little town towards the river. The big church of St Ouen has marvellous, vivid stained glass, some old, some new. Despite heavy traffic roaring by, the town has a peaceful and contented air of good living. There are excellent food shops, while the Monday and (especially) Friday markets are colourful, crowded and loaded with top-quality produce from the market gardens of the fertile marshland. There's an excellent and reasonably priced restaurant here in **Auberge du Vieux Puits** (6 Rue Notre-Dame-du-Pré, tel. 32.41.01.48), a madly pretty 17th-century inn, traditionally patterned with its exposed timbers. During my visit, nearly all the other diners were British. There are a dozen inexpensive bedrooms.

Much of the Lower Seine valley comes within the borders of the Parc Régional de Brotonne (Brotonne Regional Park), which protects the various types of terrain which flank the riverbanks. Most of the park is glorious woodland of beech, oak and pine, the heart of it being the **Forêt de Brotonne** on the river's left bank. The edges of the Brotonne Forest are 15 km north-east from Pont Audemer.

Within the woods you can walk, drive or ride beneath the shady branches. There are sights to see, too. The graveyard of the village church at **La Haye de Routot**, on the southern fringes of the forest, is home to two huge yew trees thousands of years old. There's even a chapel inside one of them, and an oratory in the other. The village is the scene of a colourful, popular annual bonfire festival on the night of 16 July. On the west side of the forest, little **Vatteville**, now set well back from the riverbank, used to be a busy port.

Pont de Brotonne, a long, high bridge built in 1977, gracefully crosses from the Brotonne Forest to the Seine's right bank. To the left of the bridge lies the small town of **Caudebec-en-Caux** (*53 km from Le Havre*). This too was once an important port, very well known before the Second World War for its wealth of lovely old houses. The Germans deliberately set fire to them. It was well known too for the tidal bore – *le mascaret*, as it was called – which used to run up the Seine and reach frightening proportions at Caudebec especially at the two equinoxes (March and September). Despite the risk, people used to assemble beside the river to see this phenomenon. Among casualties of *le mascaret* were Victor Hugo's daughter and son-in-law. The Seine bore has since been 'tamed' by engineering close to the estuary.

If you want to try to imagine how Caudebec looked before the German fire, see the three surviving medieval houses beside the 15th- and 16th-century Flamboyant Gothic church which Henri IV considered 'the most beautiful chapel in the kingdom'. A few paces from the church is the Place du Marché, where the market has been held every Saturday since the year 1390. Close by is one other fragment which survived the 1940 blaze, the gable walls of the 13th-century Maison des Templiers. Reconstructed, the building now houses the tourist office. Although no longer particularly attractive, the town has an agreeable atmosphere and a pleasing riverside setting.

Travelling upriver on the right bank (I would pass the rather overrated St Wandrille Abbey without a pause), the road gives some lovely river views in places before reaching **Jumièges** (*68 km from Le Havre*). The big, rambling and beautiful 11th-century abbey ruins beside this village are enticingly hidden away. The lovely buildings might still be standing if it were not for an enterprising merchant who bought them at auction in 1793 in order to quarry the stone. He set to work at once by blowing up the famous lantern tower, and went on to do enormous damage. Yet even what survives deserves to be seen and gives great pleasure.

Catch one of the little ferries – at Jumièges, or Duclair, for example – to drive again along the prettier left bank to **La Bouille** (*68 km from Le Havre*), an adorable little place which Monet liked. Nowadays a lot of other people like it too, and on every sunny day the citizens of Rouen flock here in their cars, which means it's not quite as Monet would remember it. Nevertheless, this is a pretty, floral riverside village in a dramatic setting at the foot of a steep wooded white escarpment. Climb the slope behind the village, on D67, to see the castle of 'Robert the Devil' (Château de Robert-le-Diable). These ruins of a 10th-century early Norman fortress – there was no such person as Robert the Devil – now contain a Viking museum and give an impressive view of the Seine; behind the château are the woods of the Forêt de Londe. There are several good restaurants (many are also small hotels) in La Bouille. Prices in this setting are on the high side, especially in places with a river view, but for visitors to Rouen this makes a tempting alternative to staying in the city, which is only 15 km away.

NORMANDY VEXIN

From Rouen to the Normandy border: about 70 km

The historic region of Vexin extended along the right bank of the Seine approximately from the confluence with the Oise (some 30 km from Paris) almost as far as Rouen. It was a border region divided by the Epte river. On one side lay the Vexin Français, with Pontoise as its capital. On the other side of the river was the Vexin Normand, hotly disputed between the French and the Anglo-Normans. The riverside route is thoroughly peaceful now, and is an interesting, attractive region of contrasting woods, farms and chalk escarpments marking the former edges of the river plain and giving stunning views.

Les Andelys (*40 km from Rouen*) is a main centre for the region. It's really two villages which have merged, Petit Andely and Grand Andely. Together they make a most pleasing small town. Grand Andely is mostly modern, but Petit Andely is a delightful place, picturesque and old, on the very bank of the Seine just where the river curves exquisitely. Islands make the river even more beautiful at this point. You can see all this from the Château Gaillard, perched above the town. *Gaillard* means 'bold', with a touch of stylish swagger, and the castle earned its name for appearance and setting, for the fact of being constructed within a year, for supposed invincibility and for its objective of announcing that 'Normandy starts here'.

monet's garden at Giverny

This imposing fortress of white stone was put here by Richard the Lionheart, the savage Crusading King of England who intended it to prevent the French from making any incursions downstream. The castle served its purpose during his lifetime, but when the throne of England passed to King John, the French began a lengthy siege. Eventually they discovered that the weak point was the latrines; climbing through these insalubrious openings, the French were soon able to seize the castle – and within a short time had moved on to take the city of Rouen for the French king. Down by the Andelys riverside, **La Chaîne d'Or** (27 Rue Grande, tel. 32.54.00.31) is an 18th-century tollhouse, now a hotel-restaurant of tremendous charm, with excellent menus served in its beamed dining room. The hotel's name comes from the chain which used to hang across the river here to bar all shipping until a toll had been paid: so lucrative was the toll that it soon became known as the 'golden chain'.

Vernon (*63 km from Rouen*), constructed as a border town by Rollo, the first Duke of Normandy, lies mainly on the left bank of the river. It has some attractive avenues and a few half-timbered houses, as well as an interesting old church and a remnant of its 12th-century castle. Cross the river and travel 4 km upriver to find **Giverny** (*67 km from Rouen*), where the leading Impressionist painter Claude Monet lived from 1883 until his death in 1926, aged 86. His house and gardens are open to the public and, despite the thronging crowds of visitors, are exquisite. The house, with its Japanese prints hanging on the walls, his photographs, his studio, the kitchen with its copper pans, look as if he might return at any moment. The gardens are magnificent, and of course one of them – with a lily pond and elegantly curved Japanese footbridge – is particularly fascinating. Monet made this garden, or the lilies, the subject of dozens of paintings during his latter years. But don't expect to see any of Monet's own works here. They are now in the world's most prestigious art museums, notably the Marmottan and the d'Orsay in Paris.

SOUTH OF THE SEINE

50 km–120 km from Le Havre

The broad agricultural plains south of the Seine are patched by forest and seamed by wooded valleys. Along the valley roads you will find interesting and attractive towns, villages, ruined castles and monastic sites, but also some industrial activity.

The Risle joins the Seine estuary soon after flowing through Pont Audemer (see p. 79). Continuing upstream, it reaches **Le Bec-Hellouin** (*37 km from Rouen*), which is set above the river with good views over the valley. The ruins of its once vast (and once vastly wealthy and influential) abbey, founded in 1034, are another reminder of the close links between Normandy and England: two of its early abbots became Archbishops of Canterbury. The best part of what remains is the 15th-century St Nicholas Tower, which has been restored. In the surviving vaulted refectory a new Benedictine abbey church has been established. Leaving the Risle and following the stream of the

Charentonne, you soon arrive at **Bernay** (*52 km from Rouen*), a busy town which preserves several fine 16th-century timbered dwellings, as well as a number of other handsome civic buildings of the 17th century.

Another enjoyable valley drive travels upriver from **Louviers** (*17 km from Rouen*), through which the Eure divides into several streams. This semi-industrial town, long associated with textiles, has an ancient quarter with several handsome old houses. Turn to join the attractive valley of the little river Iton, going as far as **Évreux** (*55 km from Rouen*), a big town which was almost totally destroyed in the last war. A resilient place, long used to war, it recovered its prosperity and its standing as a local capital. Anything that has survived from the past has been carefully restored, including the imposing church at its heart.

Take the Rouloir valley into the forests of Évreux and of Conches, to reach **Conches-en-Ouche** (*73 km from Rouen*). The little hilltop town is the nicest place in this corner of Normandy. The pleasant main street and the woodland setting give an appealing air. It's a great hunting centre, and on menus you'll see all sorts of victims of *la chasse*, including *sanglier* (wild boar). There's even a (rather awful) statue of this brave, tormented creature, standing behind the church and glowering at the view.

Inside the church there are excellent stained-glass windows of the 15th and 16th centuries. The town was proudly renamed Conches after Conques in the Massif Central. Previously it had been called Douville. Anyone who has been to the pretty mountain village of Conques will know that the magnificent abbey church there, built to house the relics of Ste Foy, no longer contains the remains of this odd child saint. In the year 1035 the local lord of Douville, a pious Crusader called Roger de Tosny, was on his way home from killing people in Spain. He came via Conques (it was a great pilgrimage stopping place) and, finding himself alone in the church, stole the saint's remains. He hurriedly returned with them to his home town, built the church of Ste Foy, and renamed the town Conches. There are some old houses near the church, while behind the town hall remnants of a 12th-century castle can be seen. The town has several good and unpretentious hotel-restaurants, specializing in down-to-earth local cooking that is well prepared – and very moderately priced.

5. THE HEART OF NORMANDY

Calvados and Orne

Getting there

The ferry (on Brittany Ferries) from Portsmouth to Ouistreham, 14 km from Caen, is the obvious approach to this area. The journey takes about 6 hours, usually with two daytime crossings and one at night (fewer in winter). The arrival port is within a short drive of every part of the region. Good alternatives would be the cross-ing from Cherbourg (see Chapter 6, 'Normandy Cotentin') or Le Havre (see Chapter 4, 'Upper Normandy'). Both are shorter than the Ouistreham route, but leave you with a drive of about 100 km (from Cherbourg) or 60 km (from Le Havre) to reach the heart of Normandy.

ALMOST everything that is most appealing about Normandy can be found in abundance in this rich heartland of the province. In its big towns, there's history and culture; along the coast, appealing little resorts which still recall the time when they were the height of elegance and fashion; while inland, it's an exquisitely rustic landscape, green and satisfying, with cows grazing in lush pasture, pretty apple orchards, thatched farm-houses and handsome manor houses. And everywhere, there's the hearty good food and civilized living for which Normandy is so well known.

Normandy, of course, has played a great role in British history. At the town of Falaise in 1027, a humble tanner's daughter bore the illegitimate son of Robert, Duke of Normandy. William the Bastard, as the child was known, turned out to be a valiant fighter and a great commander of men. In 1066 he led a fleet of war across the Channel to England, and his name was soon changed to William the Conqueror. The story is all told on the famous tapestry at Bayeux. William's Norman kinsmen became Britain's ruling class for centuries – to this very day, in fact. Nearly 900 years later, in 1944, British and Allied troops sailed the other way to conquer Normandy, freeing it from German occupation. Even then, many of the senior officers

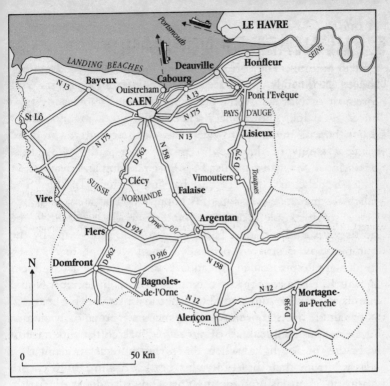

THE HEART OF NORMANDY

who led the Allied landings could still trace their roots back to the days of the Conqueror.

Inevitably, the war saw much damage done to Normandy's peaceful country towns. Much remained unharmed though, particularly away from the Calvados coast. There are many restaurants to be enjoyed in town and country, and some excellent family-run hotels. The heart of Normandy is a place to rediscover what the good life is all about. Come in spring, when all those apple trees are in blossom. Or summer, when the weather is balmy and soothing. And it's easy to get to: just step off the ferry and you're in one of the loveliest parts of France.

À *table*

All those apple trees produce not just blossom in spring and fruit in autumn. They are responsible for much good drinking. Indeed, Normandy apples are more drunk than eaten. First and foremost of Normandy's apple drinks is cider. Normandy produces no wine, and while French table wines are nowadays drunk here as much as anywhere else in the country, you'll see many a family of diners who prefer cider with their meals. Traditional Norman *cidre*, used for both cooking and drinking at table, is delicious and dry and has just a slight sparkle. The much frothier *cidre bouché*, too, is popular now as an aperitif: it's like a sort of apple champagne, and the corks are held in the bottle with a wire frame. The second contribution made by the humble apple is one of Normandy's finest accomplishments: the golden apple spirit called Calvados. Named after the département in which it is made, this is a type of brandy, a heavenly liquid fire both earthy and refined. Calvados plays a big part in Norman life, from morning – when many a Normandy workman or farmer has his breakfast of *café calva* (black coffee with a tot of Calvados) – to night, when diners finish their meals with a glassful from their best Calvados bottle. A third brew worth knowing about is Pommeau, Normandy's traditional aperitif, made from a blend of cider and Calvados. All these drinks belong to the heart of Normandy, especially to the Pays d'Auge.

Between the orchards, you'll see green fields with cows contentedly grazing. They too are vital to Normandy's gastronomy. Their full-fat milk is made into some of the best known of French cheeses: Pont l'Évêque, Livarot, Camembert and more. These are all Normandy specialities – their names are in fact villages in the Calvados and Orne départements – which to this day are better made here than anywhere else. These famous cheeses are all of the washed-rind type, and packed in little balsa-wood boxes. But locally, in the markets and village shops, you'll find many other varieties, rich, soft and creamy. Another great speciality of the region is *crème fraîche*, a thick, semi-soured cream, rather like clotted cream but with more tang and flavour. Lashings of it are used by Normandy's generous cooks, in sweet dishes and savoury, in sauces (the ubiquitous *sauce Normande* mixes cream and cider) and to accompany apple tarts, or on its own.

In short, Normans – especially in this heartland of the province – love rich food. Many a meal will start with a creamy filled savoury omelette which could stand as a main course on its own. Fish and shellfish freshly gathered from the sea are much appreciated too, and often served with a typical Normandy sauce combining cream with cider. Sole, above all, is the fish of Normandy. *Sole Normande* is made all over France, but only in Normandy, at good country restaurants, do chefs still poach the fish properly in mixed cider and cream, before adding more cream to thicken the sauce.

They'll serve you strong-flavoured meats: *andouilles* (chitterling or tripe sausage, usually eaten cold and sliced) and *andouillettes* (smaller chitterling sausage, generally served hot, with mustard), pâtés and Normandy's powerful speciality, *tripe à la mode de Caen* (a stew of tripe, trotters, herbs and cider). Caen is well known for its andouilles and andouillettes, as is Vire on the Cotentin border. The real *boudin* (black pudding) country is the Perche area around Montagne-au-Perche. In the Suisse Normande, they go in for game: pheasants, woodcock, partridges baked with apples, cream and Calvados.

Crêpes and galettes are much in evidence, whether as snacks, desserts or light main courses. But the most popular dessert is *tarte Normande*, an open flan of apples marinaded in cider (sometimes pears are used instead), and served with *crème fraîche*. So generous indeed are Norman meals, that the custom has grown up of the *trou Normand* (literally, the Norman hole!). This is a half-time break during which diners pause for a glass of Calvados, or a Calvados sorbet, before resuming their knives and forks for the next few courses!

CAEN

14 km from Ouistreham ferry terminal

A large city surrounded by industrial suburbs and a busy ring road, Caen can be daunting on arrival. Head straight into the centre though, and it is all quite manageable. In fact, the central area clusters in a square mile beside the castle. Making your way around Caen you may be surprised by the number of trees and the quantity of open space; it is known in France as one of the best examples of a *ville verte*, a green city. It's also a university town and, with about half its population aged under 25, has a lively air, with plenty of entertainment, sports facilities and popular brasseries.

Because of war damage, what was reputedly one of the most beautiful old cities of the north had to be almost entirely rebuilt. Somehow, this has been achieved with far more imagination and dignity than in many another town, and much of the rebuilding has been done in the attractive traditional material of the region, fine Caen stone. The result, if not particularly pretty, is austerely handsome. This pale honey-coloured sandstone was long exported to England – Westminster Abbey, for example, is built of it. By good fortune some of Caen's greatest historic buildings managed to survive the 1944 bombing and remain as a reminder of the city's pre-war grandeur.

They stand as a memorial, too, to the two great loves of William the Conqueror. First was his passion for his cousin, Matilda of Flanders. When he received her scornful reply to his marriage proposal – which said, so the story goes, 'I would rather take the veil than wed a bastard' – he galloped all the way to the palace of the Count of Flanders at Lille, forced his way in, and dragged Matilda around the castle by her plaits until she apologized. She not only apologized, she said she would marry him after all. His other love was the city of Caen. When the Pope excommunicated William and Matilda for marrying despite their close kinship, the matter was eventually settled by the couple agreeing to build two abbeys and four hospitals in penance. All were built in Caen, close to the powerfully defended castle which William had already constructed. William's Abbaye aux Hommes (Men's Abbey) and Matilda's Abbaye aux Dames (Ladies' Abbey) survive to this day, as does much of the castle, which dominates the city centre from its high ground.

After his own triumphant year in England, during which he had been crowned king, William returned to Matilda. The following year they travelled together to London for Matilda's own coronation as Queen of England. In 1083 Matilda died and was buried in her Ladies' Abbey; four years later William also died, and was buried in the Abbaye aux Hommes. However, his tomb, though simply inscribed in honour of this forceful Duke of Normandy and King of England, no longer contains the body: it was removed by Protestants during the Religious Wars, and then destroyed altogether by Revolutionaries.

The Men's Abbey, notably its St Étienne church, is a magnificent example of Romanesque art in its most austere mood, despite some later Gothic additions. It contains much of interest, and deserves a leisurely visit. Perhaps one of the most attractive features is the overall view of the exterior, as seen, for example, from nearby Place Guillouard.

Between the Abbaye aux Hommes and the castle, a distance of only about 800 metres, there is plenty more to see. Pass through Place St Sauveur and along little Rue aux Fromages, which have some lovely old houses, to the main shopping street Rue St Pierre. Notice numbers 52 and 54 along here: both were built in the 16th century. Arriving at Place St Pierre, you discover Hôtel d'Escoville, a grand 16th-century private mansion (it now contains the tourist office) and the church of St Pierre, built in the 14th century in a gloriously rich, highly decorated style quite in contrast to the simplicity of William's buildings.

The castle, beside the square, is in reality a well-defended citadel containing a keep. Sections of the outer walls and the keep do date back to the time of William and his son Henry, but much of the ensemble was added in later centuries. Within the walls there's a notable Musée des Beaux-Arts (Fine Arts Museum), with much Flemish and northern work, and a Musée de Normandie, dealing with the history of the region's trades and crafts and giving a fascinating insight into the daily life of ordinary people in the past. There's more to see within the castle grounds – a chapel and an exchequer, both from the 12th century, and an interesting medieval herb garden – and there are good views out across the city; just east is Matilda's Abbaye aux Dames, which unfortunately has not withstood the rigours of time and war quite so well as the Men's Abbey.

The other thing to do in Caen is spend money. This is a shopping city, with a multitude of specialist food shops and fashion stores. Many can be found near one another in Rue St Pierre and Rue St Jean, both leading off Place St Pierre. There's plenty of sensibly priced accommodation right in the centre of the city, and numerous decent restaurants. The best cooking in town, by popular agreement, is at **La Bourride** (15 Rue Vaugueux, tel. 31.93.50.76), in a splendid old house at the foot of the castle.

If you prefer to stay outside town nearer to the Ouistreham port, or if your main interest is fine eating, you may prefer the great **Manoir d'Hastings** at Bénouville (tel. 31.44.62.43), a superb hotel and restaurant in a former 17th-century priory with its own gardens, though the surrounding area – with main road passing close by – is not inspiring. The bridge crossing the river Orne at Bénouville is **Pegasus Bridge**, where the first Allied parachutists landed in advance of the great beach landings. The bar at one end of the bridge was promptly 'liberated'!

One of Caen's most impressive sights should perhaps be visited last. It deals with too serious a matter, and in too serious a way, to be encountered on first arrival. It is situated out in the suburbs; however, it is easy to find, and easy to reach. The **Mémorial pour la Paix** (Memorial for Peace, tel. 31.06.06.44) is located close to ring road N413 on the north side of town in Esplanade Dwight Eisenhower, and is well signposted coming either from the centre of Caen or from the ferry. The memorial is essentially a permanent exhibition centre which sets out to deal with the whole subject of war and peace by focusing on the cause, course and consequences of the 1944 Battle of Normandy which followed the landings. While many high-flown words and pious hopes are expressed, and there seems to be some underlying belief that war can be avoided simply through 'vigilance', the real impact of the centre is through displays dealing with the Battle of Normandy itself. The exhibition is divided into different sections each dealing with a separate aspect of the French experience of the Second World War. There are audio-visual displays on wrap-around screens in specially constructed settings, genuine archive film of wartime events is used, and no attempt is made to avoid the unpleasantness of what took place. Allow several hours for a visit.

BAYEUX

35 km from Ouistreham on minor roads, 28 km from Caen

There's much more to Bayeux than a tapestry. It's worth visiting the town simply to wander its streets and eat at one of the splendid restaurants. While you're here, though, this wonderful embroidered cartoon version of one of the greatest events in Britain's history must not be missed.

The **Bayeux Tapestry** – here known as Queen Matilda's Tapestry (although it had nothing to do with Queen Matilda, and for that matter is not even a tapestry) – is beautifully displayed around the four walls of a huge room in the Centre Culturel Guillaume le Conquérant (the former Bishop's Palace off Rue de Nesmond). It is a magnificent piece of work, 231 feet of linen embroidered with wool, depicting pictorially in minute detail the reasons for William's attack on England, how the battle progressed and how the fight was eventually won and lost. Fascinating side scenes, as well as the main story, give a unique insight into the life and customs of the people of the day on both sides of the Channel. Sometimes it verges on caricature – all the Saxons have moustaches, all the Normans have their hair cut very short at the back. If you can read Saxon dog-Latin, the original embroidered captions will make sense; failing that, make use of the tape-recorded commentary in English.

It is believed that this exceptional piece of embroidery was commissioned in England by Bishop Odon of Bayeux, who intended it to be displayed in his new cathedral. And there indeed it was displayed, or at least stored, according to the medieval cathedral records.

Odon's cathedral, built in 1077, is in Place des Tribunaux a few paces from the Centre Culturel, but only the façade and crypt remain from that date. Much of the rest is 13th century, and is a pre-eminent example of the elegant Norman Gothic

HIC WILLELM DVX ... ALLOQVITVR SV I

Fragment of Bayeux Tapestry

style. All around the cathedral are some of the most picturesque old dwellings in Bayeux, dating from the 15th century to the 18th. The cobbled main streets, the riverside walks and the air of a great past make Bayeux a delight for leisurely strolling.

The town's links with England are profound. When the Vikings, or Norsemen, first invaded this region in the 9th century, Bayeux was already in the hands of English Saxons, who had captured it from the Franks. The Norsemen conquered it in their turn, and it became the first capital of the new land of Normandy. Perhaps because of their strong control of the town, here the Vikings did not learn to speak French, and remained quite Norse in character. But many residents of the town were Saxon, and close links were formed between the two peoples. England's Saxon king, Edward the Confessor, spent many years living in the area, and named his Norman cousin William the Bastard as heir to the English throne. It was Harold's claim that Edward had changed his mind in his dying moment and named Harold instead; the Saxons in England were happy to accept this version of events, but William was not. That is what led to William's invasion of England. Part of his strategy was to weaken Harold by encouraging the Danes to attack England from the north-east: as fellow Norsemen, they were willing to co-operate to further William's ambitions.

Hôtel d'Argouges (tel. 31.92.88.86) is a reliable, middle-priced place to stay or eat. **Le Lion d'Or** (tel. 31.92.06.90) is pricier, more luxurious, and has a good restaurant, though better out of season when it is not so rushed and not so full of British visitors.

THE LANDING BEACHES

Extending west from Ouistreham ferry port for 76 km

Among the airy sands and promenades of the now peaceful little resorts on the Normandy coast there are many memories of war: of tragedy, loss and suffering, and of victory, heroism and triumph. Sections of the long Calvados seafront are still known by the names they were given during the great Normandy Landings of the Second World War, when on 6 June 1944 the Allied forces appeared suddenly at dawn, having brought over their own artificial docks, and launched the attack that was ultimately to liberate France from the Germans. The operation, code-named Overlord, was a masterful piece of daring, initiative and military strategy, and it is remembered as a superlative triumph. Nevertheless, for the soldiers themselves the experience was a visit to hell. The men arrived after a rough crossing, freezing cold, dog tired, and many were seasick. Carrying huge packs, they jumped into the water and waded ashore. They immediately came under powerful German fire, and thousands died there and then. But the advance continued. The Germans were slowly driven back from their fortifications, and on 12 August were forced into organized retreat.

At **Arromanches-les-Bains**, a fishing harbour and small-scale resort, the Musée du Débarquement (Landings Museum) tells the whole story. **Pointe du Hoc**, a small headland on the coast 2 km east of Grandcamp-Maisy, was a German look-out post which has been left exactly as it was when the fighting finished.

Yet as you drive along the little coast road today, everything is utterly calm. The beach is broad, extending to watery mud-flats in places. Locals walk on the sands gathering stranded shellfish. A flood wall cuts off the sea view on some stretches. Here and there are remnants of German defences. And there are periodic display boards graphically illuminating the events of Sword Beach (close to the Orne estuary), Juno and Gold Beaches (east of Arromanches) and Omaha Beach (west of Port-en-Bessin). The fifth main landing area, Utah Beach, lies further west on the coast of the Cotentin peninsula, and requires a longer drive (via Carentan).

Bayeux makes a perfect base from which to explore the Landing Beaches.

HONFLEUR

87 km from Ouistreham, 54 km from Le Havre

For a short visit to France at any time of year, with a chance to enjoy a little history and culture, some fine cooking and a pretty coast, as well as delightful countryside not far away (see p. 100, 'Pays d'Auge'), Honfleur is hard to beat.

This ancient seafaring town knew world renown from the 16th to the 18th centuries. It was from here, for example, and with a crew of local men, that Samuel Champlain set off in 1608 on his voyage to colonize Québec. As for the 'culture' in Honfleur, it is nothing more demanding than following in the footsteps of the great Impressionists, who made this fishing harbour on the Seine estuary one of their principal centres. From the heights of the nearby Côte de Grâce hill, with their easels facing east across the Seine estuary, the painters created scores of famous works, some of which can be seen in the Musée Eugène Boudin. The light and air and sense of space which captivated them remain the same today, even though the view has been spoiled by industry. Meanwhile the town has grown and locals are now busy catching tourists as well as fish.

But at least they *are* still catching fish at Honfleur's Vieux Bassin (Old Harbour). The port is historic and picturesque, with tall narrow buildings, dark with slate, pressed together close to the waterside. Standing guard at the harbour entrance is La Lieutenance, the 16th-century Governor's House. Waterside cafés and bars, too, contribute to the charm of the place. Artists,

Honfleur

with just an occasional one worthy of a second glance, work on the cobbled quays. There are several galleries displaying better-known painters.

Many visitors see nothing more than the waterside area, but it's rewarding to stroll into Place Ste-Cathérine, the main market square – more cobbles – to see the church of Ste Cathérine; it was constructed by shipbuilders, not masons, and the whole building is made of wood. Continue up into the attractive old town centre. Rue Haute, which stood outside the town's fortifications (demolished in the 17th century), is especially pleasing; the composer Erik Satie (1866–1925) was born at number 90.

For something inexpensive to eat, there are decent brasseries around the quays and several noteworthy restaurants. One of the best, and not especially expensive, is **L'Assiette Gourmande** (Place Ste-Cathérine, tel. 31.89.24.88). Among places to stay, **La Ferme St Siméon** (Rue A. Marais, tel. 31.89.23.61) must be mentioned if only because it was here, when it was called simply Mère Toutain, that many of the leading Impressionists, among them Sisley, Cézanne, Pissarro, Monet and local boy Eugène Boudin (whose father was an Honfleur fisherman) used to meet to drink and eat together and discuss the marvellous view. If they were alive today no doubt they would still do so, but only because their pictures now sell for millions. At the time this was a poor farm with home-made cider, simple meals and cheap basic lodgings. Now it has magnificent food, rooms from about £100 a night, and is thoroughly luxurious, superbly equipped and rather popular with Americans. More moderately priced hotels can be found in the streets around the main square.

The 15 km journey along the **Normandy Corniche** to Deau-ville gives lovely glimpses of the sea and passes through some small, enticing villages. It's best in spring or autumn; in summer this pretty coastal route can be, frankly, too busy for comfort.

CÔTE FLEURIE

*18 km from Trouville (45 km from Ouistreham, 40 km from Le Havre)
to Cabourg (26 km from Ouistreham, 59 km from Le Havre)*

The time to visit this holiday coast is high summer, preferably August, when Parisians with pretensions flock here to stroll by the sea, gamble and enjoy the racing.

A hundred years ago, the neighbouring waterfront towns of **Trouville** and **Deauville** represented the ultimate in elegance and fashion, and the other smaller places down as far as Cabourg tried hard to catch something of the same flavour. That sophistication is not quite finished, though Trouville has now a much more ordinary workaday character than Deauville.

A conspicuous proportion of the holiday makers in both resorts consists of nannies with their well-to-do young charges, even if the wealthy parents usually go further afield for their own vacation. Somehow the beachfront clings on as a sort of imitation of itself. There's a short, hectic summer season, with a busy yacht harbour, horse racing, polo, casinos, seawater spa clinics, nightclubs, chic shopping and pricey hotels. The old wooden promenade made of slats lying on the sand – called *les planches* – still gives beachside strolling a 19th-century feel. The sands are immensely wide. Yet in truth the water looks polluted and the charm of this stretch of coast has been damaged beyond repair by the sight of Le Havre's industrial port on the other side of the Seine estuary, which was once so captivatingly beautiful. Out of season, Deauville slips into a total decline, while Trouville does have an all-year-round life independent of summer visitors.

The coast road passes through a succession of less grand small beach resorts, which nevertheless do preserve an interestingly sedate and middle-class air. Almost nothing along this seashore predates the 19th century, but **Dives-sur-Mer** is older. It's the ancient port from which William set off on his mission to seize the English crown. There are still some 15th- and 16th-century buildings in the little town. Cross the river Dives to enter **Cabourg**, the well-planned but windy little resort where Marcel

Proust and his grandmother passed the summers from 1907 to
1914. Cabourg makes much of Proust now, though he was not
altogether nice about the town. The main waterfront drive is
Promenade Marcel Proust, at the centre of which is the ornate
Grand Hotel (tel. 31.91.01.79), which Proust described as a
suitable setting for a farce. Public gardens behind the hotel are
the meeting point of a semicircle of nine boulevards which
radiate through the town.

PAYS D'AUGE

About 40 km from Le Havre, 25 km from Ouistreham, 20 km from Caen

Find the river Touques on a map, flowing from Gacé, past
Vimoutiers, through Lisieux and Pont l'Évêque, and reaching
the sea at Deauville. Then find the river Dives, which flows also
from near Gacé, turns north before Falaise, and meanders towards the coast at Dives-sur-Mer. The Auge region, lying
between these two rivers, is picture-book countryside, a land of
gorgeous, satisfying rusticity. It's important to get off the main
roads, which do not show the region to best advantage. The
lanes which thread the Pays d'Auge run between little farms of
apple trees and a few munching cows, maybe a pig rooting
about in the orchard and a scattering of chickens so free-range
that when a car comes along they can't find their way back
home. There are heavily timbered traditional old farmhouses
with mouldering roofs that have flowers growing in the thatch.
Standing among the farms and villages are some houses vastly
more distinguished-looking than the rest. They are the lovely
manor houses of the Auge. Made of brick and sturdy timbers
exposed to view, these dwellings of the rural gentry are something between château and farmhouse in style. Some, indeed, do
run to château proportions.

  The farms and *fromageries* of the region produce some of the
best-known and most popular cheeses in France: Camembert
(very poor imitations of which are made in factories all over the

world), Pont l'Évêque and Livarot. All are of the type formed into small square blocks with a washed edible rind, and all are ready to eat when very soft but still springy. Pont l'Évêque, made of fresh milk still warm from the cow, has a tangy but sweetish taste. It's still nearly all farm-made. Livarot, made of skimmed evening milk and whole morning milk, has a much stronger flavour – and the smell doesn't agree with everyone. Both of these date back to the Middle Ages. Camembert was invented (or at least, brought out of obscurity) by a farmer's wife only about 300 years ago; it must be made of fresh unpasteurized milk and then cured for three weeks. When buying Camembert, always check that the label bears the letters VCN, meaning *véritable Camembert de Normandie*. Other local cheeses are of the same type: there's Pavé de Moyaux, Trouville and Petits-Lisieux, and no doubt avid investigators could discover more. The proper drink to have with all of the Pays d'Auge cheeses is not wine but another of the area's first-class products, farm-made cider. It's produced from special bitter apples which you'll see throughout the region.

In the Pays d'Auge there are two marked touring itineraries of interest: La Route du Fromage and La Route du Cidre. These lead down the rural byways from farm to farm, where the local cider and cheeses are traditionally made. Here you may sample the produce, and buy it if you wish. Of course, to do this it is not necessary to follow one of the routes. It is equally enjoyable to find your own way to the farms, exploring country roads and visiting the especially notable villages. Among them are **Beuvron-en-Auge**, a gem of a place, with an unusually large number of fine timbered houses and a decent restaurant too, called **Le Pavé d'Auge** (tel. 31.79.26.71); **Cambremer**, a plain and simple village whose name is synonymous with Normandy cider; **Orbec**, on the eastern edge of the Auge country, but one of its most handsome little towns; and **Camembert**, a tiny village with good views. Among the best of the little castles and manor houses are the one at **Grandchamp** and a smaller moated farm-manor close to it called **Coupesarte**. Several stately but rustic manor houses can be seen along the Touques valley: **St Germain de Livet**, just outside Lisieux, is a delightful

Manoir de Coupesarte in the Pays d'Auge

15th- and 16th-century castle with walls patterned in an unusual chequered brick-and-stone style; **Canapville**, between Deauville and Pont l'Évêque, is one of the most attractive manor houses.

By contrast, the main towns of the Pays d'Auge are not its most charming feature, though they are good for food shopping. **Pont l'Évêque** has some appealing old buildings at its centre, but they are collapsing as result of lorries rumbling through town. **Lisieux**, though large and partly industrial, does have an impressive cathedral and hilltop basilica. **Vimoutiers** is an important centre of the Camembert cheese trade; there's a Camembert museum here, and even a lifelike statue of Marie Harel (1781–1855) in a curious hat. She was the farmer's wife who – the inscription says – possessed the secret of making the cheese. This is more accurate than saying she invented it; something similar had been known in the area for centuries. In the towns there are a few hotels of modest standard. But *chambres d'hôte* (like bed and breakfast) are plentiful in the Pays d'Auge, offering a chance to stay in the depths of the countryside.

SUISSE NORMANDE

Starts about 25 km from Caen, 40 km from Ouistreham

It is obvious that the person who first named this pretty corner of Normandy had never actually been to Switzerland. There is not the least resemblance. True, there are hills, luscious green valleys and rich pasture, pretty rivers and a wonderful rustic tranquillity. But there's not a snow-covered peak in sight.

The heart of the area is the river Orne, as it carves a route deep through the rocky terrain which lies not far beneath the vivid green blanket of woods and meadows. To either side of the Orne repose small country towns and villages of unaffected simplicity (despite receiving their fair share of tourists). **Thury-Harcourt**, a riverside town at the northern limit of the Suisse Normande, stands on the main D562 from Caen and is perhaps the least appealing place in the whole area. However, it does have several advantages: it is easy to reach, well placed for touring, and has a selection of good restaurants and hotels.

Clécy, 10 km further south along the main road, is even better placed. It rises beside a beautiful curve in the river, and is surrounded by some of the region's loveliest country. Not only are there rewarding drives, there are also glorious walks, well signposted on the surrounding ridges and low hills. The little town has become the capital of the Suisse Normande. It has the most tempting place to stay in the whole region, the **Moulin du Vey** (tel. 31.69.71.08). It's the setting, above all, which is so seductive. In a former mill beside the Pont du Vey, greenery-draped, with a terrace running beside the river in one of its most gorgeous stretches, the Moulin is peaceful, beautiful and soothing to the soul. The mill-wheel still turns unhurriedly in the flowing water. Rooms are at least moderately comfortable, though variable, and there is a restaurant with a gloriously situated terrace. (The hotel has two splendid annexes, too: a 16th-century manor house called Manoir du Placy, and the Relais de Surosne, 3 km away.) There are a couple of cheaper places to stay within a half-kilometre. If you're just passing through, you can still enjoy the Vey waterside setting at

La Potinière, a summer-only brasserie nearly opposite the Moulin; it serves traditional home-made cider, typical Normandy crêpes and galettes, and dessert of creamy rice pudding served cold with cinnamon. This pudding, popular in North Africa and the Middle East, is surprisingly also a favourite in Normandy where it is called *teurgoule*.

Take the back-country route from Clécy to **St Christophe**, where there's another simple but delightful little hotel-restaurant which can hardly fail to please, **Auberge St Christophe** (tel. 31.69.81.23). Two kilometres beyond is **Pont d'Ouilly**, a small town at the confluence of the Noireau and Orne rivers, along both of which there are exquisite drives on tiny roads. The Orne route is arguably the more spectacular, leading to the handsome old town of **Putanges-Pont-Écrepin**. On the way the road passes between the **Gorges de St Aubert**, only accessible on foot, and **Oëtre Rock**. At a mere 120 metres (396 ft) this is the nearest thing to a mountain in the whole Suisse Normande!

SOUTHERN NORMANDY

About 70 km–120 km from Caen/Ouistreham

Along the border between the Orne and Sarthe départements, there's a certain inland warmth in the air and a feeling that the cool Channel waters have been left far behind. These southern limits of Normandy are rural, wooded and relatively free of big towns. Those which there are – lying to either side of the N12 and N176 – have a few modest attractions and serve as pleasant bases for quiet country touring. Much of the area falls within the limits of the Normandie–Maine Regional Park. There are orchards here as well though, and just for once they are of pear trees, not apple. Yet their purpose is much the same – delicious pear desserts laden with cream, and a palatable pear 'cider' called *poiré*.

The centre of the pear-growing district is **Domfront**, reached on D562 and D962 direct from Caen (*80 km*). It's an old town built along a ridge of land rising sharply from the river Varenne. Despite a busy main road at the foot of the hill, the town remains picturesque and peaceful. The streets climb to public gardens, in which stand the ruins of a fortress which was once one of the most powerful in Normandy. On the way up, you may have to turn a blind eye to the ugly modern church, but at the bottom of the hill the Romanesque church Notre-Dame sur l'Eau stands attractively beside the river, oblivious to the passing traffic. The church dates from the year 1100 and has some interesting tombs.

Bagnoles-de-l'Orne (*70 km from Caen*), hidden away beside a lake among cool, pretty woods, is not at all like the other towns of the Normandy interior. For this is a popular spa resort, with water treatments, the obligatory casino (well placed beside the lake) and masses of low-key leisure activities. Its season is strictly from 28 April to 30 September, and the rejuvenating properties of the Bagnoles waters, which emerge at a temperature of 81°F, are taken very seriously. The atmosphere of the town is sedate, restrained and slightly unreal, but it's not only the elderly who come here – Bagnoles attracts quite a lot of families with young children as well. Among the woods are lakes ideal for boating, and numerous paths for walking and riding. Several reasonable hotels can be found here and in neighbouring Tessé-la-Madeleine.

Alençon (*100 km from Caen*) is a pleasing, important and historic town, long famous for lacemaking. Although standing beside the river Sarthe, it is the capital of the Orne département. This is also the principal centre for the Normandie–Maine Parc Régional area, and is a perfect base for touring in southern Normandy and across the border in the Mayenne and Sarthe départements. For a gorgeous outing, take a country road south-west into the wonderful up-hill-and-down-dale prettiness of the **Alpes Mancelles**, just over the départemental boundary in Maine. Pause to stroll around one of the most delightful villages in the area, **St Céneri-le-Gerei** – but be warned that plenty of French tourists come here too. For that matter, it's enjoyable enough simply to stay in Alençon: there are cobbled streets, typical old timbered Normandy houses decorated with flowery window-boxes, and several impressive medieval buildings. Foremost among them is the huge 14th-century church of Notre-Dame, in exuberant Flamboyant Gothic style. The porch is especially good, and inside there's excellent stained glass dating from the early 16th century.

Close to the cathedral, the Maison d'Ozé is a handsome 15th-century mansion with fine gardens (it now houses the tourist office); Henri IV stayed here as a guest in 1576. A couple of hundred paces away along Grande Rue, the church of St Leonard is another example of the Flamboyant style. By the river at number 13 Rue du Pont-Neuf you will find the prestigious school and museum of lacemaking (Musée de la Dentelle), where you can buy exquisite examples of modern lacework, though prices are daunting. There's more lace on display at the Musée des Beaux-Arts et de la Dentelle (Museum of Fine Arts and Lace) in Rue Julien. In Place Foch, a tower and gateway survive of the medieval Ancien Château, former castle of the Dukes of Alençon. There's no shortage of moderately priced small hotels in the town. Avoid the charmless railway station area, though.

Some 40 km east of Alençon is the **Perche** region. Little known to outsiders, the Perche is a quiet land of woods, lakes and stud farms. The hard-working Percheron horse comes from this area. An interesting feature of the Perche countryside is the many fortified stone manor houses, mostly now transformed into grand farmhouses. The little 'capital' of the Perche is **Mortagne-au-Perche**, which stands atop a high escarpment with an impressive view over the surrounding country.

6. NORMANDY COTENTIN

Manche

Getting there

The most convenient arrival points for Normandy's Cotentin peninsula are Cherbourg and Caen (the Caen port is at Ouistreham, 14 km from the city). Cherbourg is at the tip of the Cotentin peninsula, and is the nearest port for every part of the region down as far as about Coutances. Further south than that, the two ports are about equally close, with some towns being a little nearer to Ouistreham. You may want to decide on the basis of what can be seen *en route*: coming from Ouistreham, you may visit the Landing Beaches, Bayeux or the city of Caen; heading south from Cherbourg, the road passes through the rustic Cotentin farm country and alongside the handsome western coast.

Journey times may be an important factor in choosing which port to use. Cherbourg is 6 hours from Southampton (8 hours at night) on Sealink; 4¼ hours from Poole on Brittany Ferries' summer-only Truckline; or 4¾ hours from Portsmouth on P&O. Ouistreham is 6 hours from Portsmouth on Brittany Ferries. For the extreme south of the département, the crossing to St Malo (9 hours on Brittany Ferries from Portsmouth) may be preferred.

WHEN Roman Polanski made that beautiful, tragic film *Tess*, which is set in the glorious old English countryside of Thomas Hardy's 'Wessex', he had to take the cast and camera crew on a Channel ferry to the Cotentin peninsula, of which Cherbourg is the bustling capital. It was the nearest place offering the perfect old-fashioned rural scenery he needed. The peninsula, defined as the area between the river Vire and Normandy's west coast, takes up most of the Manche département. It's an area of enormous charm which thrusts north from the mainland of Normandy towards the coast of Britain. Just off its western shore the Channel Islands can be seen, on the other side of the treacherous stretch of water known as the Alderney Races.

Along the multitude of lanes which thread the peninsula, farms are on a miniature yesteryear scale, with half a dozen sheep or cows in lush little pasture fields, and tiny apple orchards, enclosed by gorgeous mature hedgerows teeming with life.

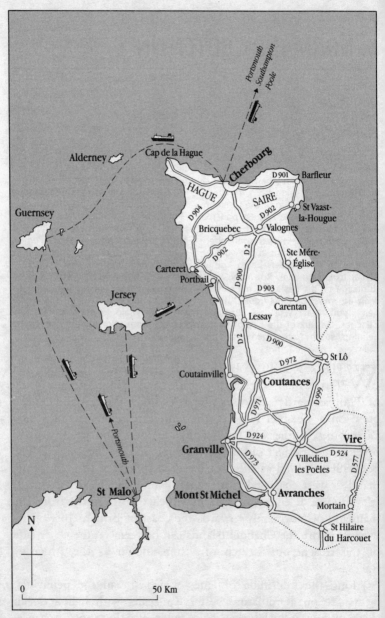

NORMANDY COTENTIN

There are pretty streams and wild flowers in profusion, and the farmland is broken up by lovely dense woods and copses of beech and oak, radiant in autumn. Heading south, the land flattens out, on the coast opening into broad sand flats backed by water-meadows. Yet around long lengths of coast, Cotentin shows another mood – harsher, rockier, more austere. There are stony fields and rocky sea-facing headlands, impressive cliffs, all interspersed with harbours large and small.

The Cotentin, unlike most of the rest of Normandy, looks resolutely out to sea. Even inland, the sea feels close. And it's here that the Vikings had the most difficulty in abandoning their old culture. Normans were first of all Norsemen, or Vikings. Owing to shortages in their own lands, from the 8th century onwards the Vikings started on campaigns of pillage and raiding throughout the whole area of the North Sea, the Channel and the Irish Sea. The Norsemen were awesome seamen, setting off to rob and rape in their high-prowed, high-sailed longships on even the stormiest of days. They were notoriously savage and terrifying, and quite indifferent to the destruction and suffering they caused. Then suddenly, in the 10th century, many of them had a change of heart. In all the lands which they had terrorized, Norsemen began to settle peacefully.

In the year 911, a Viking leader called Rollo conquered the land which was to become known as Normandy. He struck a deal with the Frankish king, Charles the Simple (who wasn't so simple after all). In exchange for being made Duke of Normandy and being allowed to settle down, with all his followers, in the territory they had won, Rollo would defend the coast from raids by other Norsemen. Rollo changed his name to Robert, and all his followers likewise embarked on an effort to live peacefully within the Frankish kingdom. The Cotentin peninsula in western Normandy had been the arrival point for many of the Vikings, and it was here that most of the ordinary men settled. Most continued to use their own language, and many place-names in this part of Normandy are still pure Norse. *Bec* in a name means a stream, *tot* is a house or farm, *hougue* means a hill or mound, *ham* a hamlet. It was barely 150 years later that, still restless and eager for conflict, many of their great-grandsons gave up their homes to set out with William on the conquest of England.

Ever since that Norman Conquest in 1066, the history of the peninsula has been closely entwined with England's. The Normans, or Anglo-Normans as they had become, were soon back in fighting spirits, and indeed William the Conqueror himself died in battle against the King of France. Dukes of Normandy vied with each other and with the French for control of both England and Normandy, and their warships made frequent landings at the harbours of western Normandy – especially Barfleur and St Vaast. The toing and froing continued through the centuries, and the Anglo-Normans became the English. During the Hundred Years War, for example, the English dominated Cherbourg and its hinterland, often landing here when heading inland on their many attempts to conquer France. During the Wars of Religion, the area was strongly Protestant and there was much contact with England. So it went on even to the present day: Utah Beach (as it was code-named), on the eastern flank of the Cotentin peninsula, witnessed momentous Allied landings at dawn on 6 June 1944. Cherbourg was a prime objective, but was not liberated for another two weeks, after heavy fighting throughout Cotentin.

Today this land is the very picture of peace and rural tranquillity. It's at a slight distance from the Normandy that most people know, and remains relatively calm, unspoiled and unvisited. It's ideal for a quiet break, enjoying the coast, the countryside and fine food.

À table

Normandy has a hearty appetite, and this part of the province is no exception. Good food, rich and skilfully prepared, served in large quantities, is the Norman way of eating. For snacks or light meals, delicious paper-thin crêpes and chunkier galettes (like waffles), with fillings either sweet or savoury, are a great favourite. Omelettes made with cream are eaten at either end of a meal. Main courses often revolve around seafood – *fruits de mer* – especially lobsters and oysters, for which the Cotentin peninsula is famous. *Demoiselles de Cherbourg* are fine-quality young lobsters. Other fresh fish, generally in mouth-watering cream-and-cider sauces, is as popular here as elsewhere in Normandy; *sole Normande* will be seen on many a menu.

The Cotentin peninsula does not live on fish alone. A particular speciality of the Manche département is lamb *de prés-salés*: that's meat from animals which have fed on coastal salt water-meadows. Of course, many of the same dishes belong here as in the neighbouring Calvados and Orne départements (Chapter 5). High-quality *andouilles* and *andouillettes* don't have far to come from Caen and Vire. *Tripes à la mode* is served here, and food stores offer all the best of Normandy farmhouse cheeses – Pont l'Évêque, Livarot, Camembert, Neufchâtel – brought in from the Pays d'Auge and Pays de Bray. There are some local cheeses as well, such as the strong soft Bricquebec from around the village of that name. Apple tart with lashings of tangy *crème fraîche* is the classic dessert. And cider goes as well with the food here, and a generous tot of Calvados just as well after it, as in the rest of Normandy.

CHERBOURG

Ferry port

Cherbourg, at the northern edge of the peninsula, is today a big modern place; but it's backed by hills, so farms and fields never feel far away. The town's old heart, clustered close to the port, remains picturesque and colourful. Much of this Quartier Central has been pedestrianized, and it's a delight to wander window-shopping, stopping to buy some of Normandy's delicious specialities, or pausing for a cake and a coffee. The British are well liked here, and, if you're short of francs, I have noticed that in some of the shops they'll even accept British money (at a very reasonable exchange rate, too).

You can get a magnificent overview of the town and its setting from the sturdy ramparts of the Fort du Roule, a fortress on the lofty summit of a cliff overlooking the harbour. Gazing down, it's easy to see how crucial this superb port must have been to the region's history. Inside the fort there's a museum devoted to the 1944 Liberation, with real maps, scale models, plans and photos – good background if you plan to visit the nearby Landing Beaches. The 1944 Allied onslaught did succeed in flushing out the Germans but subjected the town to tremendous bombardment.

After enduring so much, it's amazing how much of Cherbourg's old centre survives unscathed. The most ancient streets and alleys are medieval, with attractive stone houses which have been skilfully restored – look especially around Rue au Blé. Many other buildings date from the flamboyant 19th century – the exuberant theatre in Place Général de Gaulle is a prime example. The theatre has a constant stream of music, dance and variety shows: there's always something on. Or, for a front seat just observing life in the Place, you could relax in the pleasant and civilized **Café du Théâtre**. On Tuesday, Thursday and Saturday the Place is alive with market stalls loaded with fruits, vegetables, geese and ducks and hens, shellfish, dairy produce and brilliant flowers.

In Rue Foch, near the port, you'll find the tourist office (opposite one of Cherbourg's curiosities – an English telephone booth, with a working pay-phone inside it). Round the corner there are two good restaurants, both fish and seafood orientated, **Café de Paris** and **La Régence**, standing right next door to each other at 42 and 40 Quai de Caligny. Generally agreed to be Cherbourg's best is **Chez Pain**, at 59 Rue au Blé.

Strolling around, you'll discover many high-quality food and wine shops. In oddly named Rue Grande Rue (Cherbourg's oldest street) there are excellent charcuteries and *traiteurs* (who sell cooked meats) with enticing window displays. In fact, probably the best is Madame Peschmann's relatively old-fashioned-looking little shop at number 13. She offers best-quality cheeses cut from big rounds, as well as *cèpes* mushrooms, handmade chocolates, bottles of farmhouse cider and of course Calvados. Her counter assistant scoops fresh butter from churns and beats it into neat 500-gram blocks for customers.

For gorgeous French pastries, the best pâtisserie in town is

Salon de Thé Yvard, in Place de la Fontaine. The main shopping street is Rue Mahieu, and here you'll find Printemps, an excellent department store with three floors of fashion. If you prefer to head out to a hypermarket, the best is Auchan, about 5 km away on N13, with every conceivable type of shopping under one roof – together with bars and a self-service restaurant.

AROUND CHERBOURG

30 km radius of Cherbourg

The Cotentin was the great stronghold of Normandy's first Viking settlers. Those fierce forebears of William the Conqueror left their mark permanently on this countryside in the strangely un-French names of many of the villages of the north Contentin which are from Old Norse. The region around Cherbourg is especially redolent of this Viking past.

Take a leisurely tour round and through the gentle rustic **Val de Saire** district which lies east of Cherbourg. The Saire is a delightful little river which flows through a farming country of dreamlike rusticity. **Barfleur** (*28 km from Cherbourg*), on its coast, was once a more important resort than it is now; and before that was an important port. It's not quite true, though it is sometimes said, that William the Conqueror set sail from here on his fateful mission in 1066, but the ship came from here and picked him up at Dives. Richard the Lionheart, though, did sail from here in 1194 when on his way to be crowned King of England. Today Barfleur is a little place much liked by Normandy families and

St Vaast-la-Hougue

boating types. There's an unusual church and an attractive waterfront.

A long dike which obscures the sea view runs from here to
one of the most appealing small towns on the Normandy coast,
St Vaast-la-Hougue (*about 32 km from Cherbourg*). At St Vaast
– which locals pronounce St Va' – the **France et Fuschias** (tel.
33.54.42.26) is a thoroughly satisfying middle-priced hotel
draped in fuchsias. Inside, it has comfortable rooms and an
excellent restaurant. Much of the food they serve comes from
their own farm, 2 km away, and of course their fish and
seafood are straight from the fishing boats moored not five
minutes' walk from the hotel kitchen. St Vaast is famous for
oysters, and there's a marvellous quayside quietly busy with
fishermen and their trawlers. St Vaast's harbour is much bigger
and deeper than might be needed by a simple fishing village,
and indeed it played a major role as a harbour of war in the

various conflicts between France and England. In one of the strangest episodes, thousands of Irishmen waited here in 1692 as part of James II's plan to invade England with a combined fleet of Irish and French troops. The Catholic James had been displaced by the Protestant William of Orange, and hoped to regain the English crown. The invasion plan went totally wrong, the Catholic forces being set upon by a Protestant Anglo-Dutch force before they had even started. The Irish and French sailors would not co-operate with each other when things got tough, and the Catholic fleet was destroyed – together with James's last hope of returning to England as its king.

For a different face of Cotentin, explore the area west of Cherbourg, an ocean-battered finger of land thrusting into the Channel. This corner, known as **La Hague**, is one of the most 'Viking' parts of the peninsula, with rugged coast and picturesque farming and fishing villages. Some say it's like Cornwall half a century ago. It is fabulously pretty in places, with tiny fields enclosed by mature hedges, stone farmhouses, muddy farmyards, tiny country lanes, all within sight of the sea. The little harbour of **Port-Racine** (*25 km from Cherbourg*) along La Hague's north shore claims to be the smallest harbour in France; the claim is believable, but its neighbours are pretty small too. Just beyond is the windy **Cap de la Hague**, the furthest tip of the Cotentin peninsula. The attractive **Goury** harbour (*30 km from Cherbourg*) has its lighthouse and lifeboat at the Cap that are almost legendary for the number of lives they have saved in these rough waters. On the southern shore of La Hague the highest sea cliffs in Europe (128 metres, 422 ft) can be seen rising from the crashing waters at **Nez de Jobourg**, a headland from which there's a great panorama of awesome rock and wild waves.

South from here the coast becomes gradually gentler. The minor roads which follow the shore rise and fall sharply, sometimes giving magnificent sea views, sometimes descending to sandy coves and bays. One eyesore to be avoided, though, is the nuclear power station between Diélette and Flamanville – a pity, since this is a particularly fine stretch of coastline. Continuing

Château at Bricquebec

towards Carteret, the cliffs sink down to be replaced at last by a hinterland of sand dunes.

In the interior of the peninsula, the country changes again, opening out into a broader landscape of pasture and gorgeous woods. **Bricquebec** (*25 km from Cherbourg*) is a historic inland place dominated by a partly ruined medieval fortress. Amazingly, inside the castle there's a simple hotel and restaurant, **Hôtel du Vieux Château** (tel. 33.52.24.49). Although the rooms are variable, and Bricquebec château has not been especially famous for gastronomy, the setting has drawn in some illustrious diners. Not long ago Madame Giscard d'Estaing came for dinner. Field Marshal Montgomery, revisiting the area in 1957, came here for a meal. Most notable of all, Queen Victoria (complete with Prince Albert and various junior princes and princesses) came over from England on a private excursion on 18 August 1857. She had a room, of course, even though she merely rested and changed for dinner in it, and you can stay in it today. It has been altered since then – by the addition of a bathroom. The Queen thought the whole thing 'most amusing' (for once), even though she declared that the mayor of Bricquebec was tipsy. It's a very pleasing small town, with much old character and a big Monday-morning market.

Further south still the green pastures and cows placidly grazing present a picture of perfect rural peace.

WEST COAST RESORTS

40 km–110 km from Cherbourg

The wild rocky shores of the northern Cotentin gradually give way to a coastal landscape of sand dunes, some of them surprisingly high. The southern half of the peninsula has a succession of attractive small harbour towns and villages with beaches interpersed with rugged headlands.

The minor coast roads and the main D904 from Cherbourg run beside the dunes into the seaside resort of **Carteret** (*40 km from Cherbourg*), a delightful little fishing village on the picturesque Gerfleur estuary. Beside the harbour – from which you can catch a boat to Jersey – there's a sandy beach, and beyond it rises an attractive rocky headland called the Cap de Carteret, with a clifftop walk known as the Sentier des Douaniers (Customs Officers' Path). No doubt *douaniers* were kept busy enough here in days gone by. On the clifftop there's a lighthouse and a chapel, and on the far side of the Cap extends another sandy beach. The whole place, with its variety and old-fashioned atmosphere, has enormous appeal. Rue du Cap leads directly, by an inland route, from the old village to the Cap; a turning off, Avenue de la Roche Biard, leads to a high point with a magnificent panoramic view and a fascinating *table d'orientation* (viewing table). In addition to all that, Carteret has some good little hotels and eating places. The **Hôtel Marine** (11 Rue de Paris, tel. 33.53.83.31) has a superb restaurant and a well-placed terrace for outdoor eating and drinking beside the sea. Its rooms are not bad either.

Carteret and its neighbour **Barneville** on the other side of the estuary are technically the same place (called Barneville-Carteret), but the Barneville side is mainly quietly residential. It does have an excellent street market every Saturday, and an interesting 11th-century church, as well as a good long beach backed by the sedate Barneville-Plage development.

Portbail (*50 km from Cherbourg*), down the coast from Barneville-Carteret, is something rather similar, though smaller and little known. There's a little estuary harbour, a good beach, a handsome main square and a Romanesque church. Near the church are remains of a Gallo-Roman baptistry. Beside the beach and estuary you can enjoy good waterside walks. This is an appealing place, but with nowhere decent to stay. From here too passenger boats cross over to Jersey throughout the summer months.

It was just south of Portbail, in 1927, that Lindbergh landed in his tiny plane after the first solo transatlantic flight. The dune-backed coast for many miles beyond has no towns or villages, though punctuated by tiny beach developments reached on short access roads from D650. This is a part of Normandy with few visitors. **Lessay** (*54 km from Cherbourg*), set back 3 km from the sea on the edge of a large expanse of rough heathland, is one of the only towns in this area. It is notable for its lovely Romanesque church. When the original building, which had stood since the year 1050, was badly damaged in 1944, stonemasons using medieval tools rebuilt the damaged sections with the same golden stone as had been used before. The town also hosts one of Normandy's most historic country fairs for four days each September. Horses are bought and sold, and there's a festive atmosphere.

Coutainville (*76 km from Cherbourg, 10 km from Coutances*) is a tranquil, old-fashioned resort with a touch of faded style, though with its devotees. The beach is good, and towards the Pointe d'Agon on the big Sienne estuary it merges with wild dunes and salty marshland where waterfowl and seabirds cluster. Locals come here at low tide to look for cockles and clams.

Granville (*105 km from Cherbourg*) is bigger, more of a resort and known, too, as a spa. It's divided into two: the older Haute Ville, austere and fortified, stands on a great rocky promontory jutting into the sea; the newer Ville Basse, much larger, reaches across the lower land behind the rock. In the walled upper part of town, houses are 18th century and the streets narrow and full of character. At one end of the old town there's a huge main square, Place d'Isthme, with wide views out to sea. At the other end of the walled area rises the town's vast granite church. Part of the promontory is not within the ramparts, and there is a cliff-edge walk to be made along the Promenade du Roc, with good views. The islands you can see are the Îles Chausey, 16 km away, and in the distance beyond the Brittany coast is within sight. Descending to the livelier lower part of town with its people, shops, hotels and restaurants is like waking from a dream. From the busy port at the foot of the cliffs, frequent boats run over to Jersey and Guernsey.

The coast road (D911) continues through a succession of small resorts – **St Pair**, **Carolles**, **St Jean-le-Thomas** and **Genêts**. All are more or less appealing, with old village churches, stretches of beach between rocks and often good views across to Brittany and Mont St Michel. Here and there, though, there are also remains of German gun emplacements on the seashore. The road eventually arrives at Avranches, a busy and popular town at the southern end of the Cotentin peninsula, on the edge of Mont St Michel Bay.

AVRANCHES

125 km from Cherbourg

An agreeable little town, Avranches climbs up to the summit of a hill above the river Sée as it flows into Mont St Michel Bay. The setting is attractive, and the town itself rewards leisurely strolling in its narrow old streets and lanes. There are several good, unpretentious hotels and restaurants. Avranches is a place closely connected, in the mind and in the eye, with the great abbey just across the water at Mont St Michel. For one thing, Avranches gives two incomparable views of Le Mont: one from the vividly colourful Jardin des Plantes (Botanical Gardens), and the other, higher up in the town, from Place Daniel-Huet. In the Place there stood, until it collapsed in 1794, a great cathedral, and indeed Avranches was the seat of an influential bishopric. It was Bishop Aubert of Avranches who, in response to a vision, founded the Mont St Michel abbey in the early 8th century. In the former Episcopal Palace close to Place Daniel-Huet, the town's museum contains masses of interesting local items, including a remarkable collection of manuscripts from Mont St Michel. They date from the 8th century to the 15th.

Where the cathedral stood resembles a platform, and that is exactly what the site is called: La Plate-Forme. Quite apart from its links with the great abbey, Avranches has known several other moments of importance in its history. One of them took place on this spot. With his famous cry 'Will no one rid me of this turbulent priest?' in 1170 Henry Plantagenet caused four of his loyal knights to murder Thomas à Becket in Canterbury Cathedral. Henry was accused of the murder and, as a punishment, excommunicated, which seems light enough penalty by modern standards. In 1172, as a consequence of the intervention of the Abbot of Mont St Michel, it was agreed that Henry could be absolved if he would make penance at Avranches. Barefoot and dressed only in a simple chemise, Henry entered the church on his knees to atone, before papal legates, for the death of the archbishop. Now, on La Plate-Forme one paving stone is marked out as being the place where the barefoot Henry kneeled.

There were more bare feet at Avranches in 1639 when the town's many salt-workers revolted against the newly imposed Salt Tax. Their leader, Jean Quétil, was known as Jean Nu-Pieds (Jean Barefoot); his peasants' rebellion swept through Normandy from Avranches to Rouen. Thousands of workers joined his call to kill everyone who supported the Salt Tax, and a great deal of blood was shed before the revolt was at last put down. In our own century the town was the starting point, on 31 July 1944, for General Patton's advance across northern France, sweeping the Germans before him. There's a memorial in Place Patton, at the end of Rue de la Constitution. The whole Place is supposed to be part of the USA; even the earth and trees in the square were brought over from America!

INLAND TOWNS

50 km–108 km from Cherbourg

A land of cattle pastures and secret little rivers, the interior of the Cotentin peninsula takes its produce to market in a number of pleasant country towns. Many are just as close to the ferry port at Ouistreham (near Caen) as they are to Cherbourg. You must choose carefully, though: some Cotentin towns took a severe battering in the 1944 Liberation, and were rebuilt quickly with concrete, without much time to spare on aesthetics.

Undistinguished but bustling and congenial, and with a little marina on the river Taute, **Carentan** (*50 km from Cherbourg, 50 km from Ouistreham*) is a short distance inland from the marshy estuary of the river Douve, on the very border of the Cotentin; France's famous butter-marketing centre, Isigny in Calvados, is only 11 km away. The elegant spire of Carentan's fine Gothic church rises high above the rooftops, and makes a landmark for miles in this low-lying countryside. The arcades in Place de la République are what survives of the 14th-century market-place, and the town hall is partly 17th century. But there's little else left from the past in this ancient pre-Roman town, which suffered a hard beating during the 1944 Liberation. Hardly 10 km north-east of Carentan is **Utah Beach**, one of the Landing Beaches. American troops arriving here with tanks and what was then the most modern artillery discovered that their equipment was almost useless in this terrain cut across by tall hedges and narrow sunken lanes. Only by fighting hand to hand with the Germans and taking each hedge at a time were they able to make progress across the Cotentin peninsula.

On the other side of the peninsula, **Coutances** (*75 km from Cherbourg, 82 km from Ouistreham*) is only about 10 km inland from the west coast. Immediately likeable, it occupies a commanding hilltop position. It's been here for a couple of thousand years, and the name Cotentin derives from Coutances. Many of the most distinguished of English families can trace their origins back to this important and impressive little Norman town. At the summit, rising grandly above all else, there is an unusually attractive Gothic cathedral. You will see its three towers long before you arrive. Both outside and inside, the building has a simple elegance and repays a leisurely visit for its fine carving, old stained glass, superb arcading and the beautiful octagonal lantern tower. Originally 11th century, the cathedral was largely rebuilt in the 13th century, but since then, remarkably enough, it has survived more or less intact. A few paces away is the smaller church of St Pierre, with another striking lantern tower, this time ornate in the Renaissance style. The town's public gardens, also very close by, are delightful. At their entrance is the grand old 17th-century mansion Hôtel Poupinel, now containing a museum.

Villedieu-les-Poêles (*108 km from Cherbourg, 103 km from Ouistreham*) attracts attention first of all for its peculiar name – God's Town of Frying Pans. The prosaic yet impressive explanation is simply that the town has been for centuries noted for the manufacture of high-quality hand-crafted copper pans. Until recently all Normandy dairy farms had a big copper flagon, called a *canne*, for the new milk; these, too, were all made here. So obviously it's a busy working town, with some heavy goods traffic. Yet it has managed to preserve a historic atmosphere, with several narrow old streets, stepped alleys and ancient courtyards with traditional metal workshops. The town's main streets lead away from the 15th-century church of Notre-Dame. In Rue Général Huard there's a display on the history of the local pan-making in a copper workshop now open to visitors, with detailed guided tours. Just across the road there's an interesting museum of copperware and lacemaking (Musée du Cuivre et Maison de la Dentellière), for lace was another craft highly developed at Villedieu. Another local skill can be discovered a few yards along Rue du Pont Chignon, where there's a fascinating bell foundry, established by the Knights of St John. It's still making bells using traditional methods, and skilled craftsmen take time off from their work to give guided tours. In town-centre shops you can buy the products of all this traditional craftsmanship. Every Tuesday the big market square is filled for a busy market.

The countryside of the Sienne valley north of Villedieu is

glorious. Twelve kilometres from town, the lovely ruins of the Benedictine abbey of **Hambye** enjoy all the tranquil charm of the rural setting. The abbey has its old library, kitchen and some farm buildings, and much good Gothic architecture. Right next door there's a satisfying, simple hotel-restaurant, **Auberge de l'Abbaye** (tel. 33.61.42.19).

MONT ST MICHEL

For Mont St Michel, see Chapter 7, 'Upper Brittany'.

7. UPPER BRITTANY

Ille-et-Vilaine, Loire Atlantique, eastern Côtes d'Armor

Getting there

St Malo is the principal cross-Channel port for Upper Brittany. The crossing, from Portsmouth on Brittany Ferries, takes 9 hours by day, 10¼ hours by night, making it the longest Channel crossing to France from Britain. It is in operation from March to December only; from June to September there are day and night crossings, in the other months night crossings only.

Good alternative routes to this part of Brittany would be via Roscoff (6–7 hours from Plymouth, Brittany Ferries), Caen/Ouistreham (6 hours from Portsmouth, Brittany Ferries) or Cherbourg (6–8 hours from Southampton on Sealink; 4¼–5¼ hours from Poole on Brittany Ferries' summer-only Truckline; 4¾–7½ hours from Portsmouth on P&O).

A MAGNIFICENT coastline, appealing harbour towns, stylish beach resorts, first-rate seafood: everything about Upper Brittany seems to be connected with the sea. The region is best visited in the fine days of early summer, or else late in the season, because during the summer peak it is very crowded, while in winter it is so unvisited that hotels, restaurants, museums and attractions are all likely to be closed.

Upper, or eastern, Brittany lacks the insularity of western Brittany, and has a more open mentality, while being very conscious of its Breton history and heritage. The Bretons were, in origin, Britons; the peninsula was settled from the 5th to the 7th centuries by thousands of British Celts from Cornwall and Wales. They were devoutly religious, with a Christianity inextricably mixed with Celtic pre-Christian ideas. They considered their new homeland as two distinct places: Armor, the sea, and Argoat, the forest. Most of the new arrivals clustered along the coast, and still today Brittany and the Breton look outward towards the sea. The whole region was known as Armorica, the name given to it by the few Celts already living in this sparsely populated part of ancient Gaul. Both by the sea and in the interior, Brittany remained for centuries a region remote and

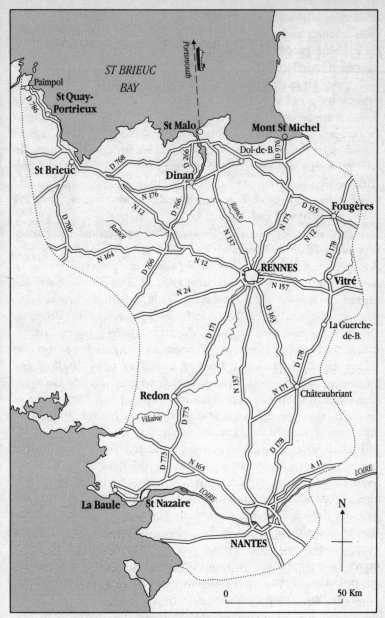

UPPER BRITTANY

undeveloped, with a people living in the narrow confines of their poverty and piety. Its native Breton rulers jealously guarded their Celtic culture against the growing power of the Frankish kingdom based in Paris.

Today, Upper Brittany is closely connected to the rest of France by good roads, airports and fast trains. The forest has been cleared – all but a few patches – and replaced by a broad landscape of agriculture interspersed with rough heath. There's a multitude of farms growing vegetables and rearing pigs. In any case this eastern half of Brittany has long been the less 'Breton' region, where the old Celtic language is not spoken and where the way of life is much influenced by neighbouring Normandy, Maine and Anjou.

In the year 843, the first Breton rebellion against the Franks was successfully led by Nominoë, who was crowned as the first King of the Bretons. The new kingdom proved unable to protect itself against the merciless raids of the Normans, and the region broke up into a mass of little counties. In the 11th century the Dukes of Normandy became Kings of England. Brittany became a subordinate duchy to these powerful neighbours, and in the 14th century a complex struggle for possession of the Duchy of Brittany sparked a war between England and France in which most Breton towns were attacked. Different claimants to the duchy continued to battle it out until Anne of Brittany, through marriage, became Queen of France. Her grandson Henri II united Brittany to France in 1547.

For all that, Brittany remained separate. The region had its own language and its own parliament of local nobles, and was granted a number of 'franchises' – rights to be exempt from French law and custom. This was the period when many of the grander Breton churches were built. The base for Breton political power was always in Upper Brittany, yet it was in this area that close contact with the French undermined the cultural differences. Not until after the 1789 Revolution (which was not much supported in Brittany) was Brittany's detachment from France officially brought to an end.

À *table*

In general, Brittany can hardly be called a great gastronomic region, although Bretons are quick to counter that charge by claiming that their fresh fish and shellfish, and lamb from the salty coastal pastures, are superb just as they are and would not benefit from extravagant preparation. They are right. Most Bretons are content with simple fare simply prepared, and the aim of top Breton chefs is to leave the best products of land and sea as near to their original state, and with as much of their fresh flavour, as possible. What sophistication there is in Breton cooking derives mainly from the influence of the Nantes area, on the borders of the more gastronomic Loire valley. In particular, the Nantes style has given Breton dishes the benefit of butter sauces.

Fish and seafood dominate the diet. There's a fantastic abundance of shellfish. Oysters, lobsters, clams, scallops and mussels are everyday fare. Eating in Brittany, you will become quite familiar with the difference between *homard* (lobster), *langouste* (smaller than a lobster) and *langoustine* (smaller still). Clams (*palourdes*) are often stuffed with chopped shallots, herbs and butter. The coasts east of St Malo, especially around Cancale, are particularly noted for oysters. The best scallops come from St Brieuc, on the other side of St Malo.

Turbot, sole, bass and monkfish are landed almost straight on to quayside restaurant tables. There are pike, eels, carp and trout, and sometimes salmon, from the clear, clean rivers of the interior. Deep-fried baby eels (*civelles*) are a speciality of the Nantes area, although fresh fish are generally served steamed or in a mild *beurre blanc* (wine-and-butter sauce), and accompanied by a few garden-fresh vegetables lightly boiled. Sometimes fish are mixed together and made into a plain stew called *cotriade*.

Of course in many eating places you'll come across Brittany's best-known speciality, *homard à l'Armoricaine* (Armorica meaning Brittany). The lobster is cooked in olive oil, flambéed and served with a sauce of cream, wine, onions, tomatoes, garlic and herbs, plus a dash of vinegar or lemon – some of which are curiously untypical ingredients for Brittany.

Upper Brittany is not quite so fish-oriented as Lower Brittany. In this more easterly part of the province, there is much fine charcuterie. Menus include *andouilles* and smaller *andouillettes* (spicy pork-and-tripe sausages). You will sometimes be offered *kig ha fars*, a rich meat, vegetable and dumpling stew. And you will see on many a Breton menu leg of lamb (*gigot d'agneau*) whose particular flavour, comes from the sheep being grazed on the salty water-meadows (*prés-salés*), near Mont St Michel. The meatiest part of Brittany, now not officially in Brittany at all, is the Nantes area, where duck with cherry sauce (*caneton aux cerises*) is a local favourite.

Many Breton specialities come from the baker's. Mostly these are cakey fruit pies and batter puddings like *far Breton, kouign-amann* and *galette fourrée*. In the crêperies (every Breton town and village has at least one) there's an immense selection of paper-thin crêpes and chunkier galettes. They can be sweet or savoury, made of white flour, wholewheat or traditional buckwheat. They are washed down with dry cider or, more traditionally, buttermilk.

For full meals nowadays wine is more usual than cider. The Loire valley wines are considered local, including of course the Nantes region's own two whites. Gros-Plant has a most distinctive dry taste, unlike any other wine. Muscadet is crisp and bone-dry, and is the ideal accompaniment to seafood.

ST MALO

Ferry port

Grandest of all the Channel ports, French or English, is the great walled town of St Malo. If you're arriving on the Portsmouth ferry, especially after the overnight crossing which cautiously approaches this difficult shore in the early-morning light, it looks quite awesome. The first sight of the town, tightly bound within tall stone ramparts rising from rock and waves, is thrilling and majestic.

St Malo stands on a headland almost completely surrounded

by water. Imposing gateways lead into a labyrinth of lanes and streets lined with high terraces of austere stone buildings. Nowadays St Malo has spread on to the mainland far beyond its curtain of fortifications, but the **Intra Muros**, as the enclosed area is called, still contains the heart and soul of old St Malo. 'Old' perhaps is not quite the word, because the whole place was painstakingly rebuilt stone by stone, with perfect fidelity to its former appearance, after being destroyed in two weeks of fire and bombing in 1944. The result is a prosperous 18th-century fortified town in mint condition. Of course, the place predates that: it was a Gallic and then a Roman harbour town, and the ramparts were put up in the 12th century before being reinforced by that ubiquitous military architect Vauban.

The 'saint' in whose honour the town is named was in fact a 6th-century Welsh settler called Mac Low. He has not been beatified, but that doesn't make much difference to the Bretons, who designate as 'saints' all their early warrior-priests.

A walkway works its way round the top of the ramparts, with spectacular sea views to one side of the path and, to the other, intriguing glimpses into the kitchens and back-yards of the terraces. It comes as a surprise, perhaps, to see people sunbathing on the narrow strip of sand below the walls. Offshore, Grand Bé island can be seen. The writer Châteaubriand (honoured in street names all over France) is buried there, under a simple unmarked tomb on the seaward side. Viscount Châteaubriand (1768–1848) was born and brought up at St Malo. Although an aristocrat, he survived the Revolution because of his own republican sympathies. He travelled widely but was essentially solitary, and requested that he be buried on this lonely island beside his native town. Only after his death was one of his best-known works published, *Mémoires d'outre-tombe* (Memories from Beyond the Grave). The island may be reached by a causeway which is exposed at low tide.

To learn more about St Malo's long past, right up to and including the wartime destruction, visit the town museum inside the waterside castle which forms part of the ramparts. The tower on the side of the castle is known as the Quic-en-Groigne, after the inscription carved on it by Duchess Anne in response

St Malo

to local opposition when she announced her marriage to Charles VIII of France. The marriage was seriously to undermine Brittany's independence, but Anne's carved message to her critics read defiantly: 'Qui qu'en groigne, ainsi sera, car tel est mon bon plaisir' (No matter who complains about it, it will be thus, for that is my good pleasure). Inside the Quic-en-Groigne tower there's now a waxworks museum depicting scenes from the town's history.

Focal points of the town, with good bars and restaurants, are Place Châteaubriand and Porte Dinan. Main streets ideal for shopping and strolling curve between them. More picturesque, perhaps, are the lanes around the little Marché, where there are colourful markets every Tuesday and Friday. (For hypermarket shopping, go to Le Continent on the south-western outskirts.)

St Malo has a long and formidable reputation as a town of pirates and privateers, adventurers and discoverers: in other words, tough characters who knuckle down to no one. Indeed, the St Malo citizen's proud motto is 'Ni Français, ni Bretons, Malouins suis' (Not French, not Breton, from St Malo am I). Despite that stance, St Malo today is staunchly Breton, with

Brittany's eatable specialities much in evidence in the pâtisseries and épiceries. There are good crêperies, where cider or buttermilk is served, and the town has some excellent restaurants. Intra Muros, try reliable little **Astrolabe** (8 Rue des Cordiers, tel. 99.40.36.82) or pricier **Duchesse Anne** (5 Place Guy La Chambre, tel. 99.40.85.33). Extra Muros – the part of town which lies outside the walls, and which from the locals' point of view is the real workaday St Malo – try the **Cap Horn** restaurant at **Le Grand Hôtel des Thermes** (100 Boulevard Hébert, tel. 99.56.02.56); the hotel itself is geared towards people on seawater health cures. For a pleasing little hotel of moderate price within the walled town, a good choice would be **Hôtel Elizabeth** (2 Rue des Cordiers, tel. 99.56.24.98).

AROUND ST MALO

About 40 km radius of St Malo

St Malo lies almost on the borders between Brittany and Normandy. This is an area of impressive and varied coastline, dominated to the east by the broad shallows of Mont St Michel Bay. It's a short and easy seashore drive from St Malo across into Normandy proper. Inland too there is peaceful countryside with many features more Norman than Breton, such as picturesque heavily timbered thatched farmhouses.

West from St Malo, across the broad Rance estuary, the deeply indented coast is punctuated by popular holiday resorts. Everywhere the seashore, varying from wild headlands to wide sandy bays, is superb, although some of the little resort towns are bland and do not impart much local character. The largest and most popular, with good beaches, good views and good restaurants, is **Dinard** (*13 km from St Malo*), just across the Rance.

Heading the other way out of St Malo, along the rugged shore which runs north-eastward, there are dramatic sea views. At the Pointe du Grouin, one craggy pointed tip of the curve of land which cradles Mont St Michel Bay, there's an immense panorama along the shores of Brittany and Normandy. There's a hotel-restaurant in this impressive location, called sensibly enough the **Hôtel Pointe du Grouin** (tel. 99.89.60.55). Just south of the point, the busy fishing harbour and oyster 'farming' centre **Cancale** (*14 km from St Malo*) has more than its share of good little eating places, notably the great **Restaurant de Bricourt** (tel. 99.89.64.76), which also gives an opportunity to see inside a *malouinière*, one of the mansions built around St Malo by its many prosperous corsairs. But you don't have to eat in such a gastronomic shrine to enjoy ultra-fresh Cancale oysters. There are dozens of simple bars on the long waterfront which can serve you a plateful with a half-bottle of Muscadet or Gros-Plant. Cancale's streets run steeply down to the port, while an imposing grey church rises above the town.

Following Mont St Michel Bay, the road looks out on a wide expanse of mud-flats and water from a succession of vantage points and through a string of sea-facing villages. A long grassy dike separates the sea from the road. Signs invite you to sample 'Moules, Cidre' (mussels, cider). Occasionally there are glimpses of the dreamlike Mont St Michel rising from the sea. **Le Vivier-sur-Mer** (*21 km from St Malo*) is noted for mussel beds, and from here there are boat excursions into the bay.

Just inland from Le Vivier, 8 km from the sea, **Dol-de-Bretagne** (*25 km from St Malo*) possesses an astonishing ensemble of remarkably old and grand dwellings. It's altogether a curious town, standing on top of what was an ocean-washed cliff when these houses were built. In fact, *dol* is Breton for a plateau or high flat ground. Long before you reach the town, you will see its massive grey Gothic cathedral St Samson rising above the rooftops. The Promenade des Douves, behind the cathedral, is a walk on the former sea-facing ramparts. It's enjoyable to stroll or stand on the promenade, gazing out across the rich agricultural plain which has replaced the sea. Rising from the midst of the fields, there's a conspicuous hill, Mont Dol, which used to be an island. However, the real highlight of Dol is the collection of magnificent houses. Grand-Rue-des-Stuarts and its continuation Rue de Jamptel are lined with wonderful survivors of distant centuries. Several date back to the 13th, 12th or even the 11th century. Some of the houses are arcaded, some timbered, most are ornate and beautiful. Numbers 17 and 18 Grand-Rue-des-Stuarts are believed to be the oldest domestic buildings in France. The ground floors of most of these ancient dwellings are now shops. So fascinating is it to wander slowly along Dol's main streets that on my last trip I forgot the time and ended up missing the ferry home!

Dinan (*30 km from St Malo*) is another inland town, large, and approached by crossing an immensely high viaduct. It's dominated by an old basilica and handsome medieval ramparts. To reach the attractive walled heart of the town follow signs to Vieux Dinan. Inside this fortified centre there are cobbled streets, lovely old houses, a great atmosphere, magnificent views and a curious oval keep standing across the ramparts. It also has an excellent and remarkably inexpensive hotel-restaurant, magnificently sited above the ramparts, **Hôtel Avaugour** (1 Place du Champ, tel. 96.39.07.49).

Two other interesting small country towns set inland from the coast are **Lamballe** (*55 km from St Malo*), with a rocky escarpment in the middle of it, and **Plancoët** (*32 km from St Malo*), with a pleasant bustle among its old stone houses.

MONT ST MICHEL

55 km from St Malo

The stupendous abbey church at the summit of Le Mont St Michel has been an important place of pilgrimage since the Middle Ages, and is still the most visited *site touristique* in France. It's the picture-book setting and perfect visual harmony of the scene, as much as the grandeur and history of the abbey, which have made Mont St Michel so popular. Even if you don't like crowds, you should make a journey to see this extraordinary granite fusion of town and mountain rising pyramid-like from a strange land-and-sea-scape of flat sands. Be here as the high tide comes rushing in across the flats – it's a magnificent, almost terrifying sight. See it on a bright still day in early summer when

Dinan

the sea, the meadows, the Mont and its motionless reflection all seem to twinkle with delight. Come on a cool, misty day as it catches the pensive light of early morning, or of evening. Visit in winter, when just a few isolated figures are wandering, rather than the coachloads of summer. Or come in July, for the pilgrimage procession which walks across the sands, or in September, for the great autumn festival dedicated to St Michel. And see it at night when there's a full moon – that's magical.

Until recently, many of the water-meadows which run out towards Le Mont from the mainland did not exist. Natural silting, together with a determined programme of land reclamation, have brought into being a considerable area of pasture for sheep. The seawater has its effect on these pastures, such that sheep grazed upon them have a distinctive taste, and *agneau de prés-salé* (lamb from salt-meadows) is a great speciality of local gastronomy.

Strictly speaking, Mont St Michel is in Normandy. The present border is drawn across the marshes to the west of Le Mont. Even using the older border, the river Couësnon, it is reached via the right bank, the Normandy side. However, it is altogether closer to St Malo than any other port, so I have included it in Upper Brittany. Besides, the Couësnon used to reach the sea a little to the east of its present course, which would have made Mont St Michel less clearly in one province rather than another!

The abbey does have its origins in Normandy, though. It was founded by the Bishop Aubert of Avranches in the year 708, although it had earlier been a Celtic religious site dedicated to the dead and then a Roman temple, taken over by Christians. In 966 Richard, Duke of Normandy, enlarged Aubert's church and established a community of Benedictines here. A village clustered round the tide-washed foot of the mount. Subsequent generations piled on yet more stone arches, pillars, steps and fortifications. The greatest expansion was in the 13th century, when King Philippe-Auguste of France, making amends for damage done to the buildings by his soldiers, constructed the huge Gothic abbey most of which survives today. Given the dignity and beauty of the place, it's hard to believe that after the Revolution it was turned into a prison, and so remained until 1874. Not until 1966 did the Benedictines move back.

Although medieval pilgrims flocked here and were rooked of every penny as they walked along the single village street leading up to the abbey, they had a much harder time making the journey than we can even imagine. The permanent causeway linking Le Mont with the mainland was not built until 1874. Until then it was often a case of making a cautious trek across the exposed sands (and quicksands) of low tide. The danger was legendary, and even features in the Bayeux Tapestry in a scene showing Norman soldiers sinking in the Mont St Michel quicksands. And it was vital to complete the crossing before the tide turned; because when it did, the waters raced across the sands at the rate of fifty metres a minute!

Nowadays it is no trouble getting to the place, though you still risk being rooked if you pause for a snack or a souvenir along the fascinating old Grande-Rue, still the only street. Climb the steps to the abbey church, and you'll also be asked for a hefty fee to go inside. It's worth it, however, to witness the sheer elegance and awesome dimensions of the building. With its terrace, cloister, refectory and ramparts, the abbey provides a vast amount to see. Allow several hours. If you do feel like a bite to eat go to **Hôtel-Restaurant Mère Poulard** (tel. 33.60.14.01) and sit down to Le Mont St Michel's greatest speciality, *omelette de la Mère Poulard* (literally, Mother Hen's omelette).

ST BRIEUC BAY

75 km–120 km from St Malo

Along the western shores of St Brieuc Bay a succession of little harbour resorts look out on to sandy bays and rocky outcrops. The bigger towns are geared up to receive large numbers of tourists. Inland, there's gently undulating countryside of arable farms.

St Brieuc (*75 km from St Malo*) is a large workaday town, yet can be a useful base during summer for touring and sightseeing or going down to the beaches. Out of season, when you are confined more to the town itself and to your hotel, it would be less satisfying. It does have some attractive old streets, though, a 13th-century fortified cathedral and plenty of good shopping. There's no shortage of decent middle-priced places to stay.

St Quay-Portrieux (*92 km from St Malo*) is very much the all-round holiday resort, with a golf course and other sports facilities, a casino, five beaches, scores of discos, bars, restaurants and hotels.

Paimpol (*117 km from St Malo*) has changed beyond recognition since Pierre Loti wrote about it in his classic novel *Pêcheur d'Islande*. But Loti has been rewarded for writing about the town by having several streets and squares named after him. On Quai Loti, there's an interesting Musée de la Mer (Museum of the Sea) telling the story of old Paimpol. Today the town has no fishing romance, merely a busy modern fishing industry, while oysters are cultivated in offshore beds. It's a lively local centre and a well-placed base for the extremely beautiful northern limits of St Brieuc Bay.

RENNES

70 km from St Malo

In Brittany's heyday as an independent duchy, its capital was Rennes, almost on the eastern boundary of the province. As the Breton parliament was here, the city became a great defender of the region's rights and identity. It's still Brittany's capital, now a large industrial, commercial and university city, an academic bastion of Breton learning. However, for the visitor, most of Rennes lacks appeal, apart from a small central area. Most of this older heart, rebuilt in solid pink granite after a huge fire in 1720, has an austere handsome dignity. Around the 18th-century core, a few streets survive which were not caught in the great fire. They have charming 15th- and 16th-century houses and mansions, which provide a picturesque setting for shopping, idling, eating and lingering in cafés.

The river Vilaine passes through Rennes, and imposing buildings line the quaysides. Close to the cathedral and the oldest streets, the river is joined by the Canal d'Ille et Rance. The waterways provide pleasant boundaries on two sides of the central quarter. Just south of the Vilaine is Rennes's important Palais des Musées (Museums Palace). On the lower level, the Musée de Bretagne (Brittany Museum) has the finest collection anywhere of material telling the whole story of Brittany and its people from the earliest times until the present day. In the same building, upstairs, the Musée des Beaux-Arts (Fine Arts Museum) has collections dating from the 16th to 20th centuries. There are some Impressionists (Sisley, Boudin, Corot) and a few canvases from the Pont-Aven group, including a Gauguin (*Oranges*). Picasso appears among more recent artists.

In a street behind the Palais des Musées is the lycée which was the scene of the notorious second trial of Captain Alfred Dreyfus in 1899. Five years earlier, the Jewish army captain

Rennes

had been falsely accused as a spy by an anti-semitic ring within the army and sentenced to deportation. However, in 1896 clear evidence emerged that Dreyfus was entirely innocent, and the identities of the anti-Jewish conspirators and the name of the real spy (Major Esterhazy) became known. A virulently anti-semitic press campaign argued against a retrial for Dreyfus, but eventually he went for a new trial at Rennes. Instead of being acquitted, as had been expected, in the Rennes court Dreyfus merely had his sentence commuted to ten years' imprisonment – a scandal which ultimately revealed the extent of anti-semitism permeating the judiciary as well as the press and the military. However, despite the Rennes verdict, the Government ordered Dreyfus to be released immediately. Not until

1906, though, did the army permit him to return. He died in 1935.

Cross the Vilaine into the heart of old Rennes. One of the landmark buildings of the town centre is the grand 17th-century former Breton Parliament, now the Palais de Justice (Law Courts), standing in a distinguished central square. The building is open to visitors. Inside, you pass through a succession of magnificent rooms and halls, of which the most impressive is the rich Grand' Chambre, the parliamentary debating chamber. Superb wood-carving and panelling cover the ceiling, and modern tapestries drape the walls; at the sides are lavish private boxes, theatre-style, from which distinguished visitors could observe the proceedings.

Close to the Law Courts in Place de la Mairie is Rennes's horseshoe-fronted town hall with its huge onion-domed clock that locals know as 'Le Gros'. Across the square is the bow-fronted theatre. Round the corner from the town hall you reach the city's most interesting and attractive church, the 17th-century St Sauveur. The cathedral stands almost next door to it, but like most of the other churches in central Rennes, while having some good features, it's not of great interest. For a moment of peace and relaxation, walk over to the attractive and extensive Jardin du Thabor, just east of the central area. There are a multitude of excellent restaurants in town. The best is **Le Palais** (7 Place du Parlement, tel. 99.79.45.01), much acclaimed, centrally located and surprisingly inexpensive.

FOUGÈRES

76 km from St Malo

Through the green and rustic farmland of the eastern edges of Brittany, the road to Fougères brings the woods and farms of neighbouring Normandy and Maine strongly to mind. The town itself is large, sprawling and outwardly rather charmless. It was always known as the place where sailcloth was made, then in the 19th century Fougères became, as it remains, a centre for the manufacture of women's shoes. Penetrating to the heart of the town, though, you find the remains of a pleasing fortified old quarter perched on the edge of an impressive ravine. The most attractive ensemble of older houses can be found in Place du Marchix.

Looking down into the ravine from the shady heights of the Place aux Arbres, you have a magnificent overview of the town's riverside castle with its mighty walls and towers. The Nançon river now flows past the fortress, but once ran right around it, providing extra protection. Though massively fortified, the castle was apparently easy to seize – probably owing to its odd situation at the bottom of the ravine instead of on the top! A succession of invaders had no trouble defeating Fougères, which as a frontier post was much wanted for its strategic position. Go down to the castle for a leisurely walk on the ramparts or a guided tour within the walls.

The town was a centre of the 'Chouans' – peasant forces who fought against the autocratic leaders of the Revolution. Victor Hugo and Balzac both wrote stirring accounts of the rebellion, and both were set in and around Fougères. The townspeople then led the rebellion against the Mass Levy (poll tax) introduced in 1793.

Fougères has a succession of trade fairs throughout the year. More interesting is the Breton music festival in January, and a summer festival in July. There's a good market every Saturday and a cattle market every Friday. One of the town's best features, at any time of year, is the beech forest a couple of kilometres to the north.

VITRÉ

90 km from St Malo

There's a splendid view of this historic border town as you approach from Fougères. Heading into the centre, you find a marvellous medieval quarter within fortifications, standing on the bank of the river Vilaine. A considerable stretch of the ramparts survives. This enclosed heart of Vitré has a pedestrian-ized zone full of interest. A sturdy triangular castle with towers and castellations, originally 13th century but altered in the 14th and 15th centuries, dominates the scene. A drawbridge and entrance fort present admirably daunting access to the interior of the fortress, in which there is, inside the Montafilant and Oratory towers, a chapel (with a beautiful 16th-century triptych) and a museum mainly of 15th- and 16th-century domestic stone carving. It comes as a surprise, though, to see the rather misplaced mock-Gothic town hall within the walls.

Walking in the old quarter you will have to pause every few minutes to admire fascinating houses. Rue de la Porterie, Rue d'Embas and especially Rue Beaudrairie are particularly reward-ing. At the end of Rue Notre-Dame stands the ornate Flamboy-ant 15th-century church, with its curious seven gables on the south side.

Incredibly, much of the old town south of the walls was knocked down to build a railway line from Paris to Brest. Fortunately the line did not impinge upon the ancient ramparts. The district north of the river is known as Rachapt ('bought back'); the name comes from the Hundred Years War, when the English, unable to take the castle, decided to sit it out on the opposite bank of the river. Time passed. The men of the castle ate, bathed and slept with their swords at the ready, while the English camp took on a permanent look. Finally the residents of the town offered to pay the English to go away – to buy back the land on which they were camped. The English consented, pocketed the cash and went off to look for other castles to attack. To get the fine overview of the castle and the town which the English enjoyed from their camp, walk along the Chemin des Tertres Noirs which runs through woods on the north bank of the Vilaine.

LA GUERCHE-DE-BRETAGNE

112 km from St Malo

This quiet little town on the border of Brittany and Maine has much to recommend it. Small and manageable, it has arcaded medieval houses around Place de la Mairie, an interesting 12th- to 16th-century church with good wood-carving and stained glass, and pleasing countryside all around. It is within an easy drive of Rennes, Vitré and Laval over the border in Maine. Any courting couple staying here during a full moon should pay a visit to the Roches-aux-Fées (Fairy Rock), in the nearby woods. This may or may not enhance their chances of a happy relationship. In fact a megalithic monument, it is the subject of many local tall stories and superstitions about love and marriage. Market day is Tuesday, and there's a modest Logis de France hotel here, **La Calèche** (16 Avenue Général Leclerc, tel. 99.96.20.36).

AROUND LA BAULE

190 km from St Malo

In the far south of Brittany, the **Guérande peninsula** lies on the right bank of the Loire estuary. Inland, it's a curious marshy landscape, most of it within the boundaries of the Parc Régional de Brière. The marshes merge with sand dunes as they reach the sea, and many pine woods have been planted to hold the dunes in place. Along the shore are busy fishing ports and small beach resorts.

Among the resorts, the biggest and best known is **La Baule**, for nearly 100 years and still today one of the most stylish and fashionable towns on the Atlantic coast. The sand dunes on the coast at this point were fixed by the planting of a pine forest in 1840. Forty years later, the construction of the town was begun, and at the turn of the century it was already becoming a great success. Between the wars it became the height of elegance. But there has been no fading of grandeur here, although of course the market is rather less exclusive than it was.

Along La Baule's 5 km seafront there's an unbroken length of sandy beach, a broad waterside promenade, a string of smart hotels and a casino. Thanks to the sheltered setting, the weather is famously mild. There are golf courses, tennis courts and masses of other sports facilities. The pine woods behind the town are ideal for peaceful, fragrant walks. La Baule's hotels and restaurants number in dozens. Some are big, like the **Hermitage** (Esplanade F. André, tel. 40.60.37.00), which is the best in town and very expensive, while many others are small, friendly and family-run.

From La Baule the coast road runs round to the Pointe de Penchâteau. This marks the start of **La Grande Côte,** some 5 km of wild rocky shore along a narrow spur of land, a great contrast to the beaches of La Baule. There are, however, small and enticing fishing harbour resorts along this shore too. Among the two most interesting are **Batz-sur-Mer** and **Le Croisic**, both of which front on to the Grande Côte on one side and the salt marshes on the other.

Travel across the weird salt pans to the fortified village of **Guérande**, an astonishing medieval town within circular ramparts. These fortifications have remained undamaged since they were built in the 15th century, although the moat has been filled in. On a plateau overlooking the salt marshes, it's a town of salt-workers and small farmers; a winter visit catches the extraordinary atmosphere of their day-to-day lives in this unusual spot. In summer, motor vehicles are barred from the walled town. The town's granite-fronted 12th- and 16th-century church of St Aubin has an imposing interior with massive pillars. There are weekend concerts in the church in July and August.

NANTES

177 km from St Malo

Nantes is a city of work and commerce, of study and science. It long ago ceased to be a place to visit for pleasure. Yet there are certainly pleasures to be found in this former Breton capital, long-time rival to Rennes. A castle, an important museum and many excellent restaurants make a visit highly enjoyable.

As préfecture of the Loire-Atlantique département, Nantes is no longer officially in Brittany (since the creation of the ingenious new administrative regions which divide up all the historic provinces). However, it is still undeniably a Breton city.

Until the Second World War, I am told, Nantes was a place of great character. The Loire fragmented into many arms here, and was joined by three tributaries. There were islands in the city centre, and a multitude of narrow lanes around the historic port. However, war damage coupled with iconoclastic planning gave birth to the blander modern city we see today — which still, however, does have an island at its centre, and is given a certain appeal by the great Loire river.

Nantes grew first as a Gallic settlement, which was taken over and enlarged by the Romans. After the Roman withdrawal, the Britons who created Brittany came here, and spent many years fighting to defend it from the Normans. In the 13th century under Duc Pierre, and again in the 15th under Duke François II and Duchess Anne, the city became the capital of their duchy. Its position on the Loire gave it close connections to the rest of France, and indeed to the rest of the world. Nantes was in consequence more cosmopolitan and sophisticated than any other part of Brittany. The cooking style – richer and more complex than in the rest of the province – perhaps reflects this.

As an Atlantic port, Nantes prospered above all from the slave trade. The wealth and ostentation of the shipowners and merchants, together with the taint of slavery, made Nantes a target of the Revolutionaries. The city suffered greatly during the Terror. The notorious Jean-Baptiste Carrier was sent to

Nantes to carry out the 'purging'. He invented the horrible *noyades* (mass execution by drowning) and took delight in loading priests and anyone suspected of not being sufficiently pro-Revolutionary on to barges in the Loire which were sunk in mid-river. He joined the crowds watching from the banks as the occupants sank beneath the water. He then dreamed up the bizarre *mariage républicaine*. Hundreds of men and women would be stripped naked in public, tied together in pairs, and drowned *en masse*. This was too much even for the Committee for Public Safety which was organizing the Terror – Carrier was recalled to Paris and himself guillotined. During his four months in Nantes he had killed over 16,000 people.

The old part of Nantes lies just north of the arm of the Loire known as Bras de la Madeleine. Everything of interest is concentrated into a small area here. The dominating feature is the ducal château, a powerful-looking edifice, originally 13th century though the existing building is largely 15th century. Its moats are now gardens, and the river which swept round it has been covered. Once very grand, this was the residence of Duke François II. Life in his day was boisterous and easy-going, and the Nantes château had the reputation of a place where the normal formalities of court life were suspended. On at least one occasion the Duke himself was thrown into the moat by high-spirited guests. Every French king from Louis XI onward spent some time here. Louis's son, Louis XII, married the Duke's daughter Anne of Brittany here. Henri IV issued his famous Edict of Nantes (legalizing Protestantism in France) from this castle in 1598. The château also contained its own prison, where probably the vilest inmate was Gilles de Rais, who was held in 1440 before his trial and execution. He was, on the surface, a pious and patriotic nobleman who fought alongside Joan of Arc and was honoured with the position of Marshal of France. It then turned out that his private pleasure was to kidnap small boys, sexually torture and then murder them. He killed an estimated 150 before being brought to justice.

Cross the moat and pass through the imposing entrance between two towers. You enter a broad open area which formerly contained buildings. Almost everything which survives is around the perimeter, clinging to the outer wall. Most of the architecture is mixed Gothic and Renaissance. Particularly attractive is the Golden Crown Tower standing next to the castle's well. Just inside the entrance is the Governor's Major Palace, with an interesting museum of Breton art and traditional dress.

Just north of the castle stands the Cathedral of St Peter and St Paul (tourist office adjacent), an odd mix of grimly austere exterior with tastelessly ornate interior. It took 550 years to complete, having been started in 1434. Its pale limestone is untypical for Brittany, where granite is the usual building stone. The nave is superb, immensely high and graceful. The tombs of Duke François II and his Duchess are a magnificent example of Renaissance sculpture.

Cross Rue Sully to reach the Musée des Beaux-Arts (Fine Arts Museum), which has a large collection of works of Renaissance and 20th-century artists, including some Impressionists and a few modern abstract painters. Walking in the old district west of the castle and cathedral, you will see many dignified (occasionally rather pompous) 18th- and 19th-century buildings.

The thing to do in Nantes is eat good food and enjoy the two excellent local white wines, Muscadet and Gros-Plant. Not only in Nantes, but in the surrounding small towns and villages, there are superb restaurants where you can do both.

8. LOWER BRITTANY

Finistère, Morbihan, western Côtes d'Armor

Getting there

The small ferry port of Roscoff, in the far west of Brittany, is ideally located for Lower Brittany. Crossings (one or two daily, three on certain days in high season) are on Brittany Ferries from Plymouth, and take 6 hours (about 7 hours at night). Some places in the south and east of the region are closer to St Malo (see Chapter 7).

LOWER Brittany, thanks to the Plymouth crossing, is surprisingly accessible considering its position at the furthest end of a traditionally rather remote region. This remoteness has enabled local customs and even the Breton language to remain vibrantly alive, as they have not done to anything like the same extent in Upper Brittany.

New main roads and new fast railway services have done much in the last five years to bring Lower Brittany more into the mainstream of French life. However, Bretons are as quick as ever to point out that they are not French. While the French are largely descended from native Gauls, mixed with colonial Romans and conquering Germanic tribes, the Breton people are almost pure-blooded Celts who migrated from Britain. Most came from Cornwall and southern Wales – two great strongholds of native British society throughout the Roman occupation. As recently as the 5th, 6th and 7th centuries, these Britons became Bretons. They were fleeing the Angles and Saxons who were marching into every corner of Britain in the wake of the Roman withdrawal.

In their new home, the Britons found much that was congenial and familiar. The landscape, coastline, climate and opportunities for fishing were much the same as in the lands they had left behind. They settled down and lived much as they had done for centuries. It is noticeable how many place names in Lower

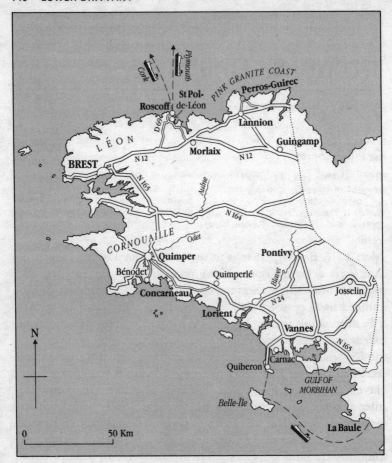

LOWER BRITTANY

Brittany resemble those in Wales and Cornwall, with plenty of examples of *Pol-*, *Tre-*, *Plo-* and *Pen-*. In Upper Brittany, there was war, intrigue and ambition. Rival Dukes of Brittany vied with other regional powers like Normandy and the Frankish kings to expand their territory or merely retain it. Meanwhile, the ordinary people of Lower Brittany continued to live, talk and think as they had always done. Learning nothing about the world except what they gleaned from Bible stories, they were village-based, each small, close community clustering tightly around its church.

The Britons were already Christians by the time of their migration here, and very devoutly so. But their Christianity was to a large degree intermingled with traditional Celtic religious ideas. Death was a central theme, and there were hundreds of revered local 'saints', who in reality were the founding priests of the community at the time of its settlement. Still today, almost every village has its 'patron saint' who is ceremonially acknowledged in the annual *pardon* – a colourful procession in which every inhabitant takes part, following an effigy or symbols of their saint. Nowadays, the *pardons* are losing their community feeling, and some of those which survive attract as many outsiders as locals. Yet they retain a powerful quality, of belief and continuity. The most popular month for *pardons*, if you hope to come across one, is September. But at any time of year old traditions and customs give Lower Brittany a unique flavour.

A feature of many villages in Lower Brittany is the *enclos paroissial* – parish enclosure. This is nothing very dramatic in some cases, and we are more accustomed to it in Britain than are the French: simply a church with a wall round it, and a village graveyard within the walls. The walled sacred grounds are entered through an elaborate gateway. However, many Breton *enclos* are spectacular, with heavily decorated Gothic churches in fantastically elaborate Flamboyant style and with a distinctive spire, and in the grounds a raised ensemble of three ornate crucifixes (called a 'Calvary'), together with an ornate ossuary, where the bones of the dead are deposited after a couple of generations have passed. The churches themselves, despite the legendary poverty of Breton peasants until recently, have had vast amounts of money lavished upon them in the form of magnificent stonework and wood-carving.

Touring from village to village in the interior is a great pleasure in Lower Brittany, where many signs remain of Breton culture. In the small bars and village shops (as often as not the bar and the shop are the same) you may well hear Breton being spoken. The countryside, which the early Bretons called Argoat,

meaning woodland, is now open and cleared, transformed into a huge patchwork of fields.

The real Brittany, though, is all about the sea. In these western fringes of the province it is especially so. The coastline varies from wild and rugged to soft and sandy. There are jagged barren rocks, or exquisitely curved sheltered bays. But whatever face the Breton coast shows, it is beautiful. While the interior may offer enjoyable tours, for a weekend base it's best to be within easy reach of the sea.

The cultural mix of French and old Breton, with hidden currents of familiarity to the British, makes Brittany an interesting place to spend a few days. However, it's not easy to visit during the winter months. From All Saints to Easter (i.e. November to March/April) almost everything is closed – museums, restaurants, hotels – and the weather is wild, windy and wet. Yet in July and August the hotels are fully booked and the roads packed. The obvious time, then, is in early or late summer, say May/June or September.

À table

Good fresh food prepared in a plain, simple way is the essence of Breton cooking. In some ways, this approach is rather like that of the British. The difference, though, is in the superb quality of ingredients which Breton cooks take for granted, and the finesse with which they retain the food's freshness and natural taste.

Brittany lives from the sea. Oysters, lobsters, clams, scallops, mussels and many another shell-covered creature which costs the earth in Paris (even more in London) are all inexpensive and commonplace in Brittany. Clams (*palourdes*) are a particular Brittany favourite, often stuffed with chopped shallots, herbs and butter. Scallops are especially associated with Brittany's westernmost coasts. Sea fish – turbot, sole, bass, monkfish – are of the highest quality, while from the rivers come excellent pike, eels, carp, trout and sometimes salmon. The fresh fish are cooked simply, generally steamed, and served with a mild *beurre blanc* (wine-and-butter sauce) and a few tasty, lightly boiled vegetables. Sometimes fish are mixed and made into a plain stew called *cotriade*.

Because of this uncomplicated style, Breton cooking has made little impact on French gastronomy. One of the few classic French dishes to emerge from Brittany, lobster (*homard*) served *à l'Armoricaine* (Armorica was the original name for Brittany), is in fact decidedly untypical of Breton cuisine. Olive oil is used to cook the lobster, which is flambéed and served with a creamy, savoury sauce made with wine, tomatoes, onions, garlic, herbs, and a dash of vinegar (or lemon). There's something odd about this dish, in that almost everything in it except for the lobster would otherwise be little used in Brittany (for example, olive oil and garlic); one wonders if the frequent misspelling *à l'Américaine* may have some truth in it, or even whether the Armor (sea) referred to was perhaps the Mediterranean!

Lower Brittany is more fishy than Upper Brittany, whence comes much of the Breton meat course. *Andouilles* and smaller *andouillettes* (spicy pork-and-tripe sausages) feature among the starters, and you may come across a rich stew of meat, vegetables and dumplings called *kig ha fars*. A leg of lamb (*gigot d'agneau*) from the sheep grazed on the meadows, submerged at high tide by salt water, near Mont St Michel (*prés-salés*) is immensely popular. Cooked *à la Bretonne*, the meat is prepared simply and served with white beans.

Inland Brittany produces excellent vegetables which are very familiar to the British palate and may seem plain and unexotic. Admittedly there are acres and acres of artichokes, but there are also huge areas devoted to cabbages, cauliflowers, green beans, new potatoes and especially onions. Roscoff has long been known as a source of onions, and the once familiar 'French onion Johnnies' were frequently straight off the boat from Roscoff. Perhaps mine is the last generation, now in our forties, to remember these solid, amiable countrymen plodding door to door in London, looking suitably foreign with beret and rosy cheeks, pushing a bone-shaker of a bicycle heavily laden with strings of big onions.

You cannot travel in Brittany – Lower or Upper – without noticing the huge number of crêperies. Nearly every village has one, often combined with other enterprises, along the lines of 'crêperie-bar-bureau de poste-alimentation' where locals come for a tasty snack, a drink, a postage stamp and to get some shopping at the same time! Crêpes are paper-thin pancakes, generally of wholewheat flour, and may be filled with (i.e. wrapped around) almost anything whether savoury or sweet. Extra-thin crêpes are sometimes called *crêpes dentelles* (lace crêpes). Equally popular are galettes. These are somewhat more substantial crêpes, usually made of wholewheat flour (*froment*) or buckwheat flour (*blé noir* or *sarrasin*). Crêpes may be served as the main course in brasseries and cheap restaurants as well as in crêperies. Special Breton bakery items, often rather heavy, can be bought at pâtisseries or sometimes seen on dessert menus: *galette fourrée* is a soft cakey fruit pie; *far Breton* is another soft cakey batter pudding with dried fruit; *kouign amann* is a round, buttery plain cake; and there are several more.

Another curiosity of Brittany's gastronomy is that old-timers, especially in the country, like to drink buttermilk or a thin, sour, yoghurt-like drink (*lait baratté* or *lait ribot*) with their crêpes and Breton cakes. With other food, Bretons are likely to drink local dry cider. Wine has caught on a lot in the last few years, and visitors are generally expected to want wine rather than cider or buttermilk. Lower Brittany cannot make its own wine, but fortunately the white wines from around Nantes in Upper Brittany – especially crisp Muscadet – are the ideal accompaniment for shellfish.

ROSCOFF

Ferry port

This must be the least known and most underestimated of the Channel ports. It's a small and charming fishing harbour and market town with a wonderfully peaceful atmosphere, a picturesque old port, streets of austere stone cottages with pretty gardens and some fine 17th-century houses with turrets. Everything is of resilient grey granite. In the main street there's a 16th-century hospital, and the church of Notre-Dame de Kroaz-Baz is Flamboyant Gothic with an elaborate Renaissance belfry; adjacent are two 17th-century ossuaries. You will also see the tower and the house named after Mary Stuart. She never lived here, but landed at the port in 1548 on her way to be formally engaged to François, son of Henri II of France. She was five years old, and her future husband in this important alliance was aged just three. They married ten years later. Six months afterwards, François died and Mary returned to Scotland – but the alliance had been achieved.

For such a remote place, Roscoff has had surprising importance, ever since 17th-century privateers – pirates who shared out their booty with the King of France – used the town as a base for their operations. Its importance today still revolves around the harbour and the sea. Brittany Ferries started their business from here, carrying not tourists but vegetables. The Charles Perez Aquarium, close to the church, not only has a fascinating collection of the underwater wildlife of the Channel, it's also an important marine research centre. There's a medical research centre at Roscoff, too, where the University of Paris studies the chemical properties of seawater.

On the quaysides there are tempting café tables. An agreeable, welcoming hotel beside the port is **Le Corsair** (Place Lacaze-Duthiers, tel. 98.61.27.28). Its rooms are well equipped and fairly quiet, and the hotel has a first-rate restaurant called **Le Temps de Vivre**. Another hotel a short distance out of town is the **Gulf Stream** (Rue Marquise-de-Kergériou, tel. 98.69.73.19). It's comfortable and most rooms have a sea view. Here too there's an excellent restaurant. For shopping, you would be better off heading into St Pol-de-Léon, 6 km away, or down to the Euromarché hypermarket at Morlaix, 28 km.

LÉON

Up to about 60 km south-west from Roscoff

The old county of Léon is the peninsula which runs westward from Roscoff and southward to the other side of the low hills known as the Monts d'Arrée. It is a bastion of Breton architecture, tradition and culture, and preserves Brittany's most striking examples of the traditional *enclos paroissial*. Churches are ornate, and belfries often have a balcony around them, almost like a minaret. Inside there's often a barrel-vaulted ceiling painted light blue, and frequently a heavily carved rood-beam (a beam running across the width of the building to give support to the roof). The Léon countryside is calm and pretty, with little hills and copses, and humble fields of vegetables.

The local capital is **St Pol-de-Léon**. It comes as a surprise on arriving at Roscoff, or even more so when returning there on the way back home, to discover that Roscoff hardly figures on road signs at all. Instead, all signs lead to St Pol, 6 km from Roscoff. Though not large, it is the biggest town (not counting the city of Brest) in the Léon district. It's a most congenial, bustling country town, one of the main agricultural markets in western Brittany. The name comes from the town's founder, a 6th-century settler from Wales called Paul; he founded a monastery on the island of Batz (pronounced 'Ba'), just offshore, later became Bishop of Léon, and was locally known as St Pol.

The town is dominated by three ornate Breton spires. Two soar from the old cathedral, while the third, the most dramatic, rises from the Kreisker Chapel, where the town council used to meet. The Kreisker spire is an excellent example of the 'open' stonework – intricate construction which leaves more open space than solid stone – typical of Breton Gothic architecture.

You may climb the Kreisker to the top, for a superb panorama of town, coast and country.

The cathedral is interesting and unusual. It has a lovely rose window, and the choir stalls are beautifully carved. Various items in the church purport to be relics of the early days of the British settlement (but it's frankly hard to know what to believe in a place as religious as Brittany). There's a tomb of the early Breton king, Conan Meriadic (died 421); and beneath a marble slab lie a head, a finger and a bone from the arm supposedly of Bishop St Pol himself. Other things which locals believe are that Bishop Paul lived to be 104 (which seems possible) and that he tied his stole around the neck of a dragon on the island of Batz and led it to a cliff, from which it jumped into the sea and was drowned (which seems a little less likely).

Wandering around town, you'll pass many distinguished mansions made of the local sturdy granite. Be here on a Tuesday to enjoy the big produce market which spills out of the main square.

Some 20 km south are several villages with fine churches in the Breton Gothic style, and exceptional *enclos paroissials* with quite astonishingly detailed and skilled stone-carving, especially in the church porches and surrounding the Calvaires. There's a marked itinerary – Circuit des Enclos – which takes you from one to another along country lanes. It makes an enjoyable outing. The villages not to miss are **Bodilis** (*28 km from Roscoff*); **Le Folgoët**, centre of a great *pardon*, adjacent to the pleasant town of **Lesneven** (*35 km from Roscoff*); **Sizun** (*40 km from Roscoff*); **Lampaul-Guimiliau** (*30 km from Roscoff*); neighbouring **Guimiliau** (*35 km from Roscoff*); and **St Thégonnec** (*30 km south from Roscoff on minor roads*).

PINK GRANITE COAST

30 km–80 km from Roscoff

This northern shore, fragmented into wild headlands and bays, scattered with tiny rocky islands, offers dramatic views. The rocks of the Côte de Granit Rose are indeed a reddish pink colour. At low tide huge expanses of sand flats are exposed, firm enough for walking or even riding. The little towns and villages, mainly dedicated to fishing, turn their hands to being holiday resorts in summer. Many of them have interesting old churches. Several of these small harbour resorts would make a peaceful retreat for a weekend away, and have small, simple hotels.

Plougasnou (*46 km from Roscoff*) is a typical small harbour of the Pink Granite Coast. It has a good little hotel-restaurant, **La France** (Place de l'Église, tel. 98.67.30.15). There's plenty of interest to see in the immediate vicinity, including superb sea views, an important megalithic site at Barnenez and a major *pardon* at neighbouring pilgrimage village St Jean-du-Doigt. The pilgrimage, the *pardon* and the name of the village are based on the gory claim, which might seem to stretch credulity beyond its limits but is widely believed, that a severed finger (*doigt*) inside the church is that of St John the Baptist.

Locquirec (*46 km from Roscoff*) and **St Michel-en-Grève** (*53 km from Roscoff*) are two charming small harbour resorts, one each side of the shallow sandy bay, Lieue de Grève. The word *grève* will be familiar to many francophiles, meaning a strike or industrial action. But it also means a wide shallow area of sands covered at high tide. The Lieue de Grève is a marvellous beach, 2 km wide at low tide, and backed by wooded slopes.

Lannion (*64 km from Roscoff*), a short distance inland, is a larger town with industry and an airport. Yet it is attractive, and at its centre has many ancient half-timbered houses and narrow, atmospheric lanes.

The coast from **Trébeurden** (*71 km from Roscoff*) right round to the big, busy port and resort **Perros Guirec** (*75 km from Roscoff by direct route*) is by far the pinkest and most granite section of this glorious coast. It is weather-beaten and infinitely varied, has appealing beaches and a coastal footpath, and is noted too for prehistoric remains. It's also, to a degree, the smartest part of Lower Brittany. Trébeurden has some excellent restaurants and hotels ranged up the hillside behind the waterfront. One of the most satisfying – yet not too expensive – is Hôtel-Restaurant **Ti Al Lannec** (Allée de Mezo Guen, tel.

96.23.57.26). Perros Guirec has many hotels, restaurants, crêperies, campsites and, of course, tourists. Yet the handsome coast beyond it, to **Port-Blanc** (*80 km from Roscoff*) and beyond, is curiously unvisited and peaceful.

BREST

63 km from Roscoff

This great capital of Lower Brittany took such a beating in the Second World War that it has never recovered. After four years of constant bombing it was taken in hand-to-hand fighting between Americans and Germans in what were left of the streets. A magnificent natural harbour, almost completely enclosed by land, had meant life to the city for centuries, but eventually was the reason for its destruction. In using Brest as a major naval base, the Nazi Germans were only following in a long tradition: every leader who hoped to control the Channel had realized the importance of Brest. Since the 17th century, it has been France's leading naval port, and it still has that role.

The city is in the old county of Léon, and it is, appropriately, a centre for the study of Celtic languages and culture. But it does not have any of that district's atmosphere and charm. The concrete-and-glass rebuilt Brest is fairly uninteresting, although the fortified harbour, now much in use by the navy, is still impressive. There are several good restaurants in the harbour quarter, and menu prices tend to be surprisingly low. But take an umbrella – Brest is known in France as the country's rainiest town!

QUIMPER

100 km from Roscoff

Administrative centre for the département of Finistère (which means Land's End), and capital of the remote old Breton district

Breton girl at festival

of Cornouaille (which is also what the French call Cornwall), the delightful town of Quimper is very much a focus for all things Celtic and Breton. Sometimes this takes a trivial form, as in the case of souvenir shops selling silly fake Breton memorabilia. But it also takes a more satisfying form as with the numerous crêperies where locals wash down their food with buttermilk or cider, the women who wear traditional clogs and shawls, and most of all with the week-long summertime Festival (or Grandes Fêtes) de Cornouaille, a chance to see full Breton dress, watch local dances and hear folk music played on local *biniou* and *bombarde* (bagpipe and flute). The festival takes place in the week ending on the last Sunday in July, and in addition to Breton music and dance you can see (very similar) performances from every other Celtic country. In all, about a thousand musicians take part.

Quimper is a most attractive and pleasing place, with agreeable squares and quaysides along the two rivers which meet here, the rather grubby-looking Odet and the sprightlier Steir. The name of the town (pronounced 'Cam-pair') comes from the Breton *kemper*, a confluence of rivers, but unfortunately the confluence itself has been covered. Locals like to believe that Quimper was founded by one King Gradlon who arrived from Cornwall in the 5th century, but in fact there was a settlement here already, and Roman traces have been found in the Locmaria quarter south of the Odet. The heart of the town now lies on the north bank of the Odet. Quimper has a congenial, easy-going quality, and an interesting air of being both cultured and rustic. There are many good food shops selling the specialities of Brittany, and I estimate that you could stay here for a month and go to a different excellent pâtisserie every single day. There's a good market every day inside the covered market-place near the cathedral. On Saturdays this becomes a wonderful street market with all the best Breton produce of land and sea.

The cathedral is memorable above all because it is built with a slight curve along its length. However, it is interesting too as one of the most complete examples of the Breton Gothic style to be seen anywhere in the province, even though it suffers from a few 19th-century changes and 20th-century stained glass. The west and south portals are Flamboyant. Between the two towers stands an equestrian statue of King Gradlon. Stepping inside the building, you notice at once the choir's slight turn to the left. There's 15th-century stained glass among the more modern windows.

Close by on the south side stands the old Bishop's Palace, with pleasant gardens and a good view. It houses the Musée Breton, with a collection of Gallo-Roman antiquities, a menhir and lots of interesting Breton furniture, costume and the fine pottery for which Quimper was long known. On the north side of the cathedral is the Musée des Beaux-Arts (Fine Arts Museum), whose collections include a few Impressionists, including Boudin's *Port de Quimper*, and several from the Pont-Aven group (see p. 162), as well as a section devoted to Max Jacob, who was a native of the town. Jacob's family home was in Rue du Parc. A Jew, he was taken by the Germans to their Auschwitz death camp along with the rest of his family. The main Odet bridge has been named in his honour.

Quimper makes an enjoyable base for a long weekend. It has good restaurants, with Breton specialities and modestly priced menus. The best in town is **Le Capucin Gourmand** (29 Rue Réguaires, tel. 98.95.43.12). In the same street there's a reliable middle-priced hotel, **La Tour d'Auvergne** (13 Rue Réguaires, tel. 98.95.08.70).

CORNOUAILLE

Around Quimper, about 100 km from Roscoff

The peninsula of which Quimper is at the head, together with some of the coast and hinterland of the mainland behind the peninsula, is called Cornouaille. It does have a remarkable resemblance to England's Cornwall, from which most of its settlers came. Like Cornwall, Brittany's Cornouaille turns its face towards the sea. It has marvellous coastal scenery, but the interior is less interesting. Small waterfront fishing villages of gaunt granite and whitewash have a neat, appealing appearance. In some of the far-flung towns you're likely to see traditional dress being worn quite casually by some of the local people, and hear Breton language being spoken.

Highlights of the peninsula are the remarkably well-preserved small town of **Locronan** (*17 km north from Quimper*), with its cobbled streets and square stone houses; the **Pointe du Raz** (*50 km west from Quimper*), a wild headland which is the Land's End of this French Cornwall; and the picturesque fishing harbour town of **Audierne** (*35 km west from Quimper*).

The Pays Bigouden is a little area within Cornouaille, with the likeable town of **Pont-l'Abbé** (*20 km south from Quimper*) as its focus. Traditional customs and dress have stayed alive in the Bigouden district. Even today you may see women, perhaps at a *pardon* or other festive occasion, wearing their old-fashioned tall and lacy white head-dress. Catch the full flavour of rural Brittany at Pont-l'Abbé's big weekly market on Thursdays. On the sheltered Anse de Bénodet bay – part of the Bigouden coast – the village of **Loctudy** (*26 km south from Quimper*) is pretty but popular. Across the bay is **Bénodet** (*15 km from Quimper*), a charming if overcrowded place with a marina and three fine beaches. Not surprisingly, it's one of Lower Brittany's busiest resorts, and there are many Britons (not Bretons) on camping holidays here. It attracts huge numbers of yachting enthusiasts, too, who give the place a certain style and cachet. Folk festivals take place throughout the summer months, and the local *pardon* is on 3 September.

Along the 'Cornish coast' south of Quimper, beyond Bénodet, there's great coastal scenery varying from wild and rocky to (more often) warm and sandy. Around the dune-backed fishing village resort of **Beg-Meil** (*20 km south-east from Quimper*), another British favourite, the seashore alternates sand and rock. Inland from here, among a mass of apple and cherry orchards, **Fouesnant** (*15 km south-east from Quimper*) has a name for strong local cider.

THE SOUTH COAST

125 km–200 km from Roscoff

The varied southern coast, much of which may be considered part of Cornouaille, attracts many package-holiday visitors. There are sandy beaches, rugged rocky shores, picturesque old waterside towns and excellent seafood. But you'll have to brave the crowds.

Concarneau (*125 km from Roscoff*) is an important local centre with a big fishing fleet, whose catch is sold by auction at a covered quayside market. It's also a tourist trap with a dreamily impressive fortified medieval quarter which is actually an island situated between the Arrière-Port and Avant-Port (Rear and Forward Ports). This curious district, called the Ville Close, is protected not only by the surrounding water but by mighty granite ramparts. Inside the walls, there are souvenir shops and a rather phoney air of self-conscious history. There's a folk festival here in July, and the lively, colourful Fêtes des Filets Bleus (Festival of Blue Nets) in August, which draws large crowds. This festival started as a religious ceremony to bless fishing boats and fishing nets, which always used to be blue (Brittany's 'spiritual' colour). The town has dozens of inexpensive restaurants – most seem to specialize in fish stew. One which is a cut above the rest is **La Douane** (71 Avenue A. Le-Lay, tel. 98.97.30.27), a friendly, lively bistro-style place a few paces from the waterfront.

Pont-Aven (*130 km from Roscoff*) is synonymous with a whole movement in Post-Impressionist art. It's not difficult to see what enticed the painters of the late 1880s to this village at the head of the Aven estuary. It is as pretty as a picture and so is the setting. As their pictures show, local people wore full traditional dress. Above the village you can see water-mills; there's a delightful wood called Bois d'Amour (Love Wood), and an exquisite chapel. One of the most prominent artists to set up his easel here was Paul Gauguin, who spent most of 1888 lodging at a cheap hotel and working on religious and folkloric themes. At one stage he offered a canvas free of charge to a local priest to hang in the church. The offer was turned down, presumably because the priest did not like the picture. It was *The Vision after the Sermon*, now worth a fortune. A group of fellow Post-Impressionists gathered in his wake, but the irascible Gauguin was repelled by the newcomers and decided to quit Pont-Aven for smaller **Le Pouldu**, about 22 km down the coast towards Lorient, where the coastline is deeply indented with estuaries noted for oysters. There, by his own account, Gauguin 'walked about like a savage and did nothing at all'. The locals did not like Gauguin or his set. The artist brawled, argued, affronted their morality and consorted with his mistress, a strange woman who carried a monkey on her shoulder. At Pont-Aven, children threw stones at them. At Concarneau, he got into a fight with some fishermen and ended up in hospital.

Lorient (*150 km from Roscoff*), a large working port of modern aspect, has little to recommend it except, first, the location on a magnificent estuary and, secondly, the big, cheerful, noisy and

Pont-Aven

colourful Festival Interceltique which lasts ten days every August. It's a great gathering of the music and dance from all of the 'Celtic nations', including, of course, Brittany.

Set back from the sea, the town of **Quimperlé** (*138 km from Roscoff*) is a jewel of pretty medieval houses, shady squares, cobbled lanes and riverside quays in a lovely valley setting. The name, like that of Quimper, comes from *kemper*, meaning a river confluence, and the two streams which join here are the Isole and Ellé, uniting to form the Laita.

The rivers make a sort of moat around the lovely old Ville Basse (Lower Town), which is, in effect, an island. Rising above all at the centre of this medieval quarter is the curious 11th-century church of Ste Croix. Essentially circular, almost entirely Romanesque, though with Renaissance later addition, it is closely based on the Holy Sepulchre church in Jerusalem. Close by, narrow little Rue Dom-Morice is lined with especially attractive 16th-century houses. Cross the Isole to climb steps to Quimperlé's Upper Town. At its summit stands the town's other church, called either Notre-Dame de l'Assomption or St Michel, built in the 13th and 15th centuries in more typical Breton

Gothic style. Two good places to eat: **Le Bistro de la Tour** (2 Rue Dom-Morice, tel. 98.39.29.58), furnished with antiques, serves delicious and imaginative well-prepared food, accompanied by decent Loire wines, all at incredibly low prices; and **Ty Gwechall** (4 Rue Mellac, tel. 98.96.30.63), where you choose a complete meal of crêpes and a *bolée* of cider, in a Breton ambience of low beams and dark antiques – again at a most manageable price.

CARNAC AND QUIBERON

204 km from Roscoff to Quiberon

One of Europe's most spectacular megalithic (Stone Age) sites is at **Carnac**, on Brittany's south coast. What you find there is simply two huge arrangements of standing stones in long dead-straight lines, although some form a big semicircle around the hamlet of Le Ménec, adjacent to the village of Carnac. They are called the Alignements du Ménec and the Alignements de Kermario, and can be found on the northern outskirts of Carnac village. There are also dolmens and a major burial earthwork partly taken over by Christians and named St Michel Tumulus. This stands right on the edge of Carnac village. From the two alignments you can take minor roads D119 or D196 to see other tumuli and arrangements of standing stones within a short distance. It all can be visited on guided tours.

Altogether the alignments comprise over 4,000 stones, some weighing 350 tons. What were they for? The question cannot be answered; the people who put them here have been dead for three or four thousand years. Of course, there are theories, notably the predictable notion that the stones had religious significance. The writer Gustav Flaubert, impressed by the stones but not by the explanations as to their purpose, wrote his own 'theories' on the subject. Perhaps, he suggested, they were giant tent-pegs.

A large number of important archaeological finds made here are displayed in the prehistory museum at Carnac. Next door to

the museum there's an interesting 17th-century church dedicated
to St Cornély, the Bretons' patron saint of horned cattle (*corne*
means horn). **Carnac-Plage**, 3 km away, has a gently sloping
sandy beach backed by pines, with hotels and holiday villas
among the trees.

The whole area around Carnac is dotted with similar but
smaller prehistoric sites. A narrow isthmus, hardly wider than
the road, connects Carnac to the Presqu'île de Quiberon
(Quiberon Peninsula), where there's an alignment of twenty-one
stones and a stone circle. The western side of the Presqu'île,
called the Côte Sauvage, is dramatic with wild rock and cliffs.
At the furthest tip of the peninsula, the small sardine-fishing
harbour town of **Quiberon** has a sheltered sandy beach and
attracts quite a number of holiday makers from June to August,
but far fewer at any other time of year. There are several rather
overpriced hotels, and ferries run from Quiberon to Belle-Île-
en-Mer, 15 km away.

BELLE-ÎLE-EN-MER

*204 km from Roscoff to Quiberon plus 15 km by ferry from Quiberon
to Belle-Île*

The name says it all: beautiful island in the sea. This haven just
offshore from the Presqu'île de Quiberon has long exerted a
strong appeal for writers, artists, and all who love to play
stylishly at the simple life in a picturesque setting.

At just 18 km long and up to 10 km wide, this is the largest
of the Breton islands. It fascinates the eye and delights the heart
with its amazing variety of scenery and landscapes, like a succession of cameos or miniatures: gaunt rocky cliffs battered by the
ocean, delicious little sheltered sandy coves, sparse pine woods
with glimpses of the sea, lush vegetation which clusters in the
valleys, a mighty fortress and charming little harbours. The
rockier coast is the glorious Côte Sauvage on the south-western
side, pock-marked with caves where seabirds nest. On the other

side, the island has gentle beaches perfect for a swim or sun-bathe.

Impressionist painter Claude Monet used to come here, as did the musician Albert Roussel. The actress Sarah Bernhardt bought a fort near the magnificent Pointe des Poulains on the island's northern tip to use as a summer retreat. The main town, barely more than a village out of season, is **Le Palais**. From the impressive citadel, originally 16th century but reconstructed by Vauban, there are superb views of town and sea. Heading north, you soon reach **Sauzon**, a pretty little harbour village colourful with flowers. A little beyond it is the panoramic Pointe des Poulains and Bernhardt's fort. Turning down along the island's west coast, one of the curiosities is the Grotte de l'Apothicaire (Apothecary's Cave), so named because the cormorants used to arrange their nests in neat rows on the shelves of rock, like jars in an old-fashioned chemist's shop. The cave runs down into the sea, catching a blue reflection from the water. Further south, there are a couple of menhirs, named Jean and Jeanne; the myth is that they were young lovers turned into stone (by whom?) for wanting to meet before their wedding day – a story which gives a small insight into traditional Breton life. Nearby on the coast there are three beautiful indentations into the rocky shore: Port Goulphar, Port Donnant and Port Coton.

The island attracts many summer visitors, but is perhaps at its most satisfying slightly out of season when there are few out-siders and the resident population of fishermen and small farmers can be seen quietly getting on with their work. Ferries to Belle-Île from Quiberon make the crossing about eight times daily between Easter and All Saints (March/April to 1 November), four times daily for the rest of the year. The journey lasts about 45 minutes. To take a car is extremely expensive, but pedestrians travel for a fairly modest charge. Ferries arrive at Le Palais, where bicycles and mopeds can be hired.

A luxurious hotel, magnificently situated and with an excellent restaurant, is the **Castel Clara** at Port Goulphar (tel. 97.31.84.21). It's a member of the Relais et Châteaux federation. There are several less expensive places. Two which are well placed and have good restaurants are **Le Phare** (tel. 97.31.60.36) at Sauzon and the **Grand Large** (tel. 97.31.80.92) at Port Goulphar.

VANNES

140 km from St Malo, 200 km from Roscoff

Vannes has a long history. Two thousand years ago it was capital of the Veneti, who were the most powerful Celtic tribe in Armorica. Caesar defeated the Veneti after a battle which, unusually for the Romans, was waged on water – none the less, the Romans were the victors, and the Veneti were transported into slavery. The settlement was taken over by the incoming Britons, and in the 9th century the first Breton king, Nominoë, chose Vannes as his capital.

Now a big harbour town at the head of the fabulously scenic **Gulf of Morbihan** (*mor bihan* is Breton for 'little sea'), the great advantage of Vannes for the visitor is its natural setting. The gulf is an intricate environment of islands and water. There are boat tours, or individual islands can be visited by ferry. About forty of them are inhabited. The largest of them, **Île des Moines** (Monks' Island), is a wonderful little place with an extraordinarily mild climate: oranges and lemons, palms and mimosas grow here. The island has a picturesque little village with some accommodation for visitors who require nothing more than peace and quiet. Several islands have megalithic monuments, and a part of the gulf is a bird sanctuary. Fishing boats throng the waters. At low tide, the water level drops considerably, and great mud-flats are exposed. A road tour around the perimeter of the gulf is interesting and enjoyable.

Vannes itself also has considerable charm. As with many other old French (or Breton) towns, the modern area is industrialized and unattractive, while the picturesque centre, close to the port, has been carefully protected. The old quarter, closed to motor vehicles, is a walled town containing much fine medieval architecture. At its heart rises the cathedral, combining Gothic and Renaissance styles. It was started in the 13th century and not completed until the 19th. All around are streets with the most striking buildings. Notice especially Place Henri IV, almost next to the cathedral. It has a marvellous ensemble of 16th-century gabled houses. The archaeological museum, housed in the 15th-century Château Gaillard, is significant for its collection of prehistoric material from Carnac and other megalithic sites around the Morbihan gulf.

Vannes has many hotels in all price brackets, and several good restaurants, among which **Le Richmont** (Place Gare, tel. 97.42.61.41), under the chef Régis Mahé, especially deserves a visit. But before ordering a bottle of Vannes's local wine, made on the Rhuys peninsula on the southern side of the Gulf of Morbihan, bear in mind this description of the wine and its merits: To drink a glass of Vin de Rhuys you need four men and a wall; one man to pour it, another to drink it and two men and a wall to keep the drinker on his feet.

JOSSELIN

105 km from St Malo, 185 km from Roscoff

One of the few Lower Brittany towns of interest which is not near the sea (the Morbihan Gulf is 42 km away), Josselin is a delightful old small town. It stands beside the river Oust in picturesque countryside. A glorious, fairy-tale castle rises from the riverbank. There's a lovely view of it from the Oust bridge. The mighty outer wall with its four sturdy round pepperpot towers was built (on the ruins of an older castle) in the 14th century by Olivier de Clisson, known as the Butcher of the English. It doesn't look quite as it did then, when there were nine towers and an inner keep (dismantled on Richelieu's orders in 1629), and no road running at the foot of the castle wall. In those days, though, no Englishman would have looked on it with leisurely admiration, for in fact the aspect would have been awesome to any foe. Within the walls, it is just as impressive. The inner façade is superb, in Flamboyant style, with skilful decorative carving of dormer windows and parapet. The highlight of the interior of the building is a superb 16th-century fireplace.

Olivier de Clisson was the son of a remarkable woman. Olivier's father was falsely accused of betraying France in the War of Succession; he was beheaded and the head displayed on the ramparts at Nantes. His devoted wife went to Nantes with her children and, in a solemn vow to the severed head, swore that she and her children would exact revenge on the French. With 400 loyal men, she attacked six French châteaux and slaughtered every occupant. Then she took to sea and sank every French ship her party encountered. Young Olivier, accompanying her on these missions, grew up to be fierce and merciless. At first he fought on the side of the English in order to continue his mother's wish to kill as many Frenchmen as possible. But reaching maturity, he joined the French army and unleashed his energies against his former allies.

Behind the castle, old houses climb a steep ridge to cluster around the church of Notre-Dame-du-Roncier, inside which is the impressive mausoleum of Olivier de Clisson and his wife Marguerite de Rohan. The castle passed to Marguerite's family, and remains in the Rohan family to this very day.

There's a market every Saturday, and on the second Sunday in September each year there is a *pardon*. The village attracts coach tours in high summer, so is best avoided then, although these visitors all go away in the afternoon, allowing overnight guests to enjoy the place in peace. There are a couple of decent, inexpensive hotel-restaurants, **Hôtel du Château** (1 Rue Général de Gaulle, tel. 97.22.20.11) and **Hôtel du Commerce** (9 Rue Glatinier, tel. 97.22.22.08).

9. MAINE

Mayenne, Sarthe, parts of Maine-et-Loire and Loir-et-Cher

Getting there

This region is within an enjoyable drive of several ports. The two nearest are St Malo and Caen (Ouistreham). Cherbourg and Le Havre are a little further away, although (adding driving time to sea voyage) the total journey time via Cherbourg, using a crossing from Poole or Portsmouth, is about the shortest.

Given such choice, the preference for one Channel route rather than another may depend on the length and price of the crossing, the quality of service offered by the ferry operator, time of arrival, the starting point in Britain and what there is to see *en route* from the arrival port to the borders of Maine.

St Malo is 9 hours by day, 10¼ hours by night, from Portsmouth on Brittany Ferries, March to December only. From June to September there are day and night crossings; in other months, night crossings only are operated, arriving at 8.15 a.m.

The Caen ferry port is at Ouistreham, 14 km from the city. Ouistreham is 6 hours from Portsmouth on Brittany Ferries. There are usually two daytime crossings and one at night (fewer in winter). Overnight crossings arrive at 6.30 a.m.

Cherbourg is 6 hours from Southampton (8 hours at night) on Sealink; 4¼ hours from Poole on Brittany Ferries' summer-only Truckline (5¼ hours at night); or 4¾ hours from Portsmouth on P&O (7½ hours at night). Sealink overnight ferries arrive at 9 a.m., P&O at 7 a.m., Truckline at 6 a.m. There are usually about two crossings daily from Portsmouth, three or four from Poole and one or two per day from Southampton.

Le Havre is 5¾ hours from Portsmouth (7 hours at night) on P&O, with usually three crossings daily. The overnight crossing arrives at 7 a.m.

ALL its neighbours are well known and much visited, but the old county of Maine has been quite forgotten. Despite the size and importance of its capital Le Mans, and the powerful historic links between Maine and England, this is a region virtually unknown to the British. It's a land of rivers, with beautiful valleys all strikingly different from each other in character. Away from Le Mans and the handful of other busy market towns, this is an exceptionally rural region of green hills, plateaux, wooded valleys and hard-working old-fashioned farming communities. Of course, visitors to Le Mans, with its medieval

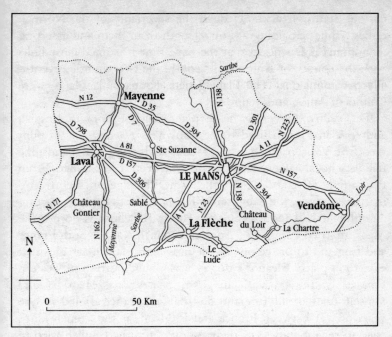

MAINE

central quarter, will have plenty to occupy them (don't go to the city during the 24-hour car race in June, though, unless that is a special interest). The rest of the region is for those who like to eat, drink, relax and enjoy a little leisurely country sightseeing. It would make a good break in summer, since the land is lush and satisfying, the weather is warm and pleasant, and even at that time of year there are relatively few visitors.

The county of Maine originally encompassed the present-day Sarthe département and most of Mayenne, but Maine does not have recognizable borders today, and perhaps never did (in this chapter I have followed the Loir valley over the border into the Loir département). The county came into being in the 10th century as a buffer zone between the predatory new Duchy of Normandy and the warlike Counts of Anjou. But William the Conqueror soon took possession of Maine, giving the county a curious status. It acknowledged the suzerainty of the Norman dukes, while remaining at arm's length from them and asserting its nominal independence; at the same time it formed close links with the county of Anjou to its south, the two counties eventually becoming one. The Plantagenets, Kings of England, were Counts of Anjou and Maine.

The yellow flowering heath plant called broom in English and *genêt* in French used to be known as *plante à genêt*. Count Geoffroi V of Anjou (1113–51) was a dashing and handsome fellow who always sported a sprig of broom in his hat. From this simple affectation came the name Plantagenet. Geoffroi V married Matilda, the daughter of Henry I of England, so starting an influential alliance. Their son, Henry II, who was born in Le Mans, married Eleanor of Aquitaine, which was for both France and England to prove one of the most important marriages that ever took place. Eleanor's dowry was a huge portion of western France. Uniting it with his own possessions, Henry found himself ruler of all England and half of France. It led to 300 years of war between France and England, as the French kings tried to regain control of their country, and the English tried to prevent them. The struggle culminated in the Hundred Years War, when the English looked set to take the whole of France into their domain. At the last minute, thanks to the inspired fervour of Joan of Arc, the fortunes of the French changed and the English were driven out of France.

Throughout the centuries, the county of Maine was invaded and attacked by many opposing factions, yet it has always been a difficult area to conquer. The English and the French fought it out here with particular bitterness during the last stages of the Hundred Years War, the English managing to cling on to Maine until halfway through the 15th century. Not until 1481 did the Plantagenets altogether lose their native soil of Maine and Anjou to the French crown. During the French Revolution, Maine was a bastion of royalism, seeing fierce fighting between the anti-revolutionary 'Chouans' and the republican 'Bleus'. Although the Revolutionary forces eventually defeated all their opponents, Maine remained loyal to the old system until the turn of the 19th century. Crucial battles of the Franco-Prussian

War in the 1870s were fought here, as were others in the Second
World War. For all that, Maine appears calmly unaffected by
these conflicts, and retains its air of detachment and rustic
tranquillity. Much of the northern part of the region now comes
within the borders of the Normandy–Maine Regional Park.

À table

Its position as a border region between Normandy and the Loire
is reflected in the gastronomy of the Maine. The charcuterie of
southern Normandy is much appreciated, but Maine makes its
own meaty preserves, too, in the form of *rillettes*, potted meats.
These are usually made of pig meat, but goose or rabbit can also
be used. Le Mans has its *boudin blanc*, 'white pudding', soft pork-
fat sausages with eggs and herbs, while the whole area around is
noted for its plump pullets and capons (*chapons*), which are
sometimes cooked in cider. Maine's green pastures feed cattle
for beef rather than milk, and this is reflected in the local menus.
The best of Normandy cheeses do not have to be brought far.
However, from the Port-du-Salut monastery near Entrammes in
the Mayenne valley comes the excellent cheese called Entrammes
(it used to be called Port-Salut, but that's now the brand name
for a mild factory-made cheese). With so many rivers, not
surprisingly freshwater fish are also a great speciality. These too
are made into pâtés and preserves, as well as being served fresh.
Eels are popular, in stews and other dishes. Maine produces
excellent hazelnuts, chestnuts and walnuts, which may appear
anywhere in the meal. There are plenty of eating apples here,
particularly of the Reinette variety, and apple desserts like *tarte
tatin* are a favourite of the area. Le Mans is particularly good for
pâtisserie and desserts. Some cider is made on the farms of
Maine, as is *poiré* (pear cider), especially in the northern parts of
Maine close to Normandy. Vineyards grow on the *coteaux*
(slopes) of the river Loir between La Flèche and Vendôme,
while the grander wines from the nearby Loire valley are also
considered to be 'local'.

LE MANS

164 km from Caen/(Ouistreham), 215 km from St Malo (*via Rennes*),
219 km from Le Havre, 284 km from Cherbourg

People think Le Mans is a big industrial town with a race-track.
And they are quite right. Thousands of visitors go to the town
for those two reasons alone – either to do business at the many
important trade fairs, or to attend motor races, especially the
world-famous 24-hour race in June. But there is much more to
Le Mans than that. From Pont Yssoir, which crosses the river
Sarthe just below the city centre, you can take in a stirring view
of the old quarter and its ramparts, and the awesome cathedral
rising over all.

The compact medieval heart of this city is a delight. Vieux
Mans, as it's called, is clustered on a hill rising from the left
bank of the Sarthe. Ancient Gallo-Roman ramparts still enclose
the narrow streets, courtyards and alleys, many now occupied by
little shops and restaurants. You'll need to park the car outside
the walls. There are car parks by the river, or alternatively above
the old town in the shady esplanade beside Place des Jacobins,
where many roads meet at the centre of the city.

The Place makes a good starting point for a leisurely look
at Le Mans. It's right in the shadow of the strange Cathédrale
St Julien. This vast architectural hybrid, with its bulky paired
flying buttresses cluttering much of the exterior, is like a cross
between pedigrees of different breeds. It does have some superb
features, but there is a question as to whether they fit well
together. Others may feel that this combination of Romanesque
and Gothic is attractive. The building's diversity reflects Le
Mans's history, hinting at the amount of conflict and violence –
and so, reconstruction – since the cathedral was first built 900
years ago.

For a closer look, walk up the steps from the Place des
Jacobins into Place St Michel, which runs alongside the cathedral. (On the left is a Renaissance house in which lived Paul
Scarron, a 17th-century satirical writer whom Le Mans is proud
to remember as a native of the city. He was the husband of

Le Mans Cathedral

Madame de Maintenon, Louis XIV's mistress.) Passing the 12th-century south doorway, go round to the lovely untainted Roman-esque west front. On the right-hand corner of the west front, a pink sandstone menhir (Celtic standing stone) has been incorpor-ated into the building. The odd legend persists that if visitors do not put a thumb into a hole in the stone they will forget their visit.

Entering the cathedral, you can see just what a jumble of styles it is. The nave is Romanesque, but with early Gothic arches which were added later; the glorious soaring chancel is perfect, elegant Gothic, and illuminated by magnificent stained-glass windows of the 13th century; while the transept is different again, and less impressive. On the north side of the transept are two grand Renaissance tombs, one of them being the grave of Charles I of Anjou.

Within the walled old quarter, there's a tremendous atmos-phere in the narrow streets, where half-timbered 15th-century dwellings stand shoulder to shoulder with fine Renaissance houses. Many of the grander mansions have distinctive names. Facing the cathedral entrance, for example, the present-day Episcopal Palace is a 16th-century mansion called Hôtel du

Grabatoire. Stroll along Grande Rue, off Place St Michel, and you'll see several other striking examples. Maison de la Reine-Bérengère at numbers 11–13 is late 15th century (it now contains a museum of history and ethnography, with some good local pottery); almost opposite at numbers 18–20, Maison des Deux-Amis is 15th- century. Crossing over the junction with Rue Wilbur-Wright, Grande Rue continues with Maison du Pilier Rouge, a half-timbered house which is now the tourist office. Wander along the other old streets to see many more of these dignified 15th- and 16th-century *hôtels*.

Outside the walled quarter, modern Le Mans offers plenty more to see. There are several interesting old churches around the town. Just off Place A. Briand, for instance, the church of Notre-Dame de la Couture, together with the present-day départemental administrative offices, occupies the buildings of a former monastery; further out by Place George Washington, the church of Ste Jeanne-d'Arc used to be a hospital, founded in 1180 by Henry II as part of his atonement for the death of Thomas à Becket. It's well worth driving 4 km out of town to the 13th-century Cistercian abbey of Notre-Dame de l'Epau, on the banks of the river Huisne. Much of the original building survives. Richard the Lionheart's wife Queen Berengaria is buried in the church, and altogether the setting makes an agreeable escape from the city's traffic. You might wish to come here in any case to enjoy one of the concerts which are often put on in the abbey.

There are several acceptable town hotels in Le Mans, some with very good restaurants. One which comes into that category is the **Concorde** (16 Rue Général Leclerc, tel. 43.24.12.30).

MAYENNE VALLEY

From Mayenne (122 km from St Malo, 127 km from Ouistreham) to Le Lion d'Angers (203 km from St Malo, 204 km from Ouistreham, 101 km from Le Mans)

The deep and winding valley of the Mayenne is richly green, a

landscape of extensive woods and unkempt pasture. The countryside seems full of hidden folds and corners, in which nestle
quiet, rustic farming villages. The resemblance is more to Normandy than the Loire. There are just a few larger towns, and all
of them have comfortable little family-run hotels at modest
prices. At the top of the Mayenne valley, flatter, less featured
country extends away in both directions.

The river runs wide through the centre of **Mayenne** (*74 km
from Le Mans*). The town climbs up steep valley slopes, giving
good views across from one side to the other. Mayenne had to
be largely rebuilt after a crucial Second World War battle. It is
an old place, though, and a few remnants do survive from its
past. Most notably, there's an 11th-century castle, with impressive outer walls, on a ledge with a commanding river view.

The drive southward from Mayenne is not the prettiest part
of the valley, but it improves close to **Laval** (*63 km from Le
Mans*), the département's biggest town. Though large and industrial, Laval is likeable. Its old heart clusters at the foot of the
castle on the right bank of the broad Mayenne. Across the water
newer districts can be seen. Originally dating from the 11th
century, the present castle was built mainly in the 13th and 15th
centuries, apart from the earlier crypt and the keep with its
curious timber roof arranged like a cartwheel. Inside the château,
among other items of interest there's a museum of naïve painting,
named in honour of Henri Rousseau, pioneer of this type of
painting, who came from Laval. Old streets next to the castle are
lined with overhanging half-timbered houses and Renaissance
stone buildings. Grande Rue runs down to the riverside quays
and the 13th-century Pont-Vieux (Old Bridge), where the view
of old Laval is especially fine. There are several good cheap
places to stay in town. One of the best is **La Gerbe de Blé** (83
Rue V. Boissel, tel. 43.53.14.10), all in traditional style and with
an excellent restaurant. Another noted restaurant is **Le Bistro
de Paris** (67 Rue du Val-de-Mayenne, tel. 43.56.98.29), where
first-class menus are amazingly inexpensive.

Just south of Laval, a short distance down the turning for
Entrammes, is the Cistercian abbey of **Notre-Dame de Port-
du-Salut**. Here the original Port-Salut cheese, now factory-made

of pasteurized milk, was invented. It was unusual among French cheeses, and that was because the monks who devised it had come here from Switzerland. Eventually they sold the trade name Port-Salut, but carried on making their cheese on the premises, using milk from their own cows. It was renamed Entrammes. There's now a proper cheese factory adjoining the abbey, and it's hard to decide whether the brothers are monks or company directors.

D112 meanders over gently undulating farmland on the river's right bank, through many bucolic scenes. At last it reaches **Château Gontier** (*80 km from Le Mans*), a big, busy town, yet pleasant, with attractive streets in its old quarter on the Mayenne's right bank. The focal point is the church of St Jean, an 11th-century building with a lovely Romanesque façade. Inside, it has a solid simplicity, with substantial stone pillars and a soothing, harmonious atmosphere. Beside the church, on former priory grounds, there's a little shaded park called the Bout du Monde (End of the World). A walkway up here gives superb views over the river and its once busy quays. On the far side of the river can be seen the more modern parts of town, though on that side there are other interesting old churches. The town's market-place is busy on Thursdays, when calves with pleading eyes are bought and sold in huge numbers.

South of the town the country is noted for horse breeding, and scattered among the farms are occasional homely old châteaux worthy of a pause. For the most part, these are not Renaissance châteaux of the Loire valley type, and only a few are built of the white tufa which typifies the Loire châteaux. The main town for this district is **Le Lion d'Angers** (*84 km from Le Mans, 22 km from Angers*), a little agricultural centre on the river Oudon just a couple of kilometres from the Mayenne. The town's ancient church of St Martin retains some good Romanesque features. Beside the Mayenne, the *haras* (breeding stud) of Isle-Briand, a modern establishment with eighty stallions, is open for visits.

Cross the Mayenne to visit the splendid white château of **Le Plessis Bourré**, standing surrounded by its wide moat in isolation amid the flat meadows. The moat has to be crossed by a long low bridge, and the exterior has a stylish fortress-like structure. Inside it's grand but comfortable, and many kings and queens stayed in this perfect little 15th-century country mansion.

A dozen kilometres south the Mayenne joins the Sarthe on the outskirts of the city of Angers (see Chapter 10).

SARTHE VALLEY

From Le Mans to Sablé: 80 km

The Sarthe flows through a wide, open valley, a bright landscape varied with woods, fields and quiet villages. There are often lovely views of the river and rustic countryside. There are few towns of any size.

Noyen (*30 km from Le Mans*) climbs in tiers from the river (and parallel canal), giving a good view over the rooftops to an island in midstream. **Malicorne** (*32 km direct from Le Mans*) has a moated Renaissance château, entered across an ornate bridge. Local hand-made pottery, long a speciality of the town, can still be seen in many shops. After reaching **Parcé** (*42 km from Le Mans*), a small town climbing up from the river, cross over to the right bank for a prettier route to **Avoise**, 2 km further. Turn up towards **Asnières-sur-Vègre** (*44 km from Le Mans*), where the older part of the village is attractive with its little bridge and a small Romanesque church with remnants of medieval frescoes.

The grimly imposing Benedictine abbey of **Solesmes** (*51 km from Le Mans*), looming up from the Sarthe riverbank, is one of the few places left where you can hear Gregorian plainchant (other than on the recordings of it – which were made here). In summer it attracts coachloads of visitors, but out of season is tranquil. Within the austere grey walls, the monks' church is dark and atmospheric. There's a good hotel-restaurant more or less opposite the abbey, **Grand Hôtel** (16 Place Dom-Guéranger, tel. 43.95.45.10). It has a garden, and the food is excellent.

Sablé-sur-Sarthe (*52 km direct from Le Mans*) is the largest town between Le Mans and the Loire. Its name is famous in

France for a kind of dry but buttery, sweet, thin circular biscuit. Everywhere in France these *sablés* are factory-made, but here pâtissiers offer them freshly baked on the premises. The main street is the beautifully curved Rue Carnot, and there are some grand Renaissance façades to be seen. The Sarthe and its tributaries trickle all over town, which gives the place a most appealing quality.

ERVE VALLEY

From Sillé-le-Guillaume to Sablé-sur-Sarthe: 56 km

The Erve is hardly a river at all, never getting much above the size of a stream, so this is not one of Maine's great valleys. In an unknown region this is an especially unknown corner. It happens, though, to be exquisitely pretty, and the little river flows through some of the greenest and most pleasant farmland of the region, passing close to several interesting villages as well.

The Regional Park of Normandy–Maine extends as far south as the lovely woodlands around **Sillé-le-Guillaume** (*33 km from Le Mans*). The name, of course, causes amusement among the British. The 'William' (Guillaume) was tacked on to Sillé in honour of the Conqueror after he had seized the town and its strategic castle. In every battle for control of this region, attention would focus on the fortress at Sillé; the handsome castle which today clings to the rocks was built in the 15th century on the ruins of the original. The main interest of the little town is as a base for the regional park and wooded Coëvron hills in which the Erve has its source.

Following the country lane, D143, which runs beside the river, you pass the dignified façade of the moated 16th-century granite castle of Foulletorte. D143 continues to **Ste Suzanne** (*45 km from Le Mans*), dramatically located on a hilltop, and enclosed by ramparts. The medieval village, now surrounded by newer developments, is perched above the Erve with a glorious, idyllic view over the river and the green countryside. Like Sillé, Ste Suzanne was a key stronghold of northern Maine. But here William failed to conquer; the site proved too much for him. Within the walls there are remnants of a 17th-century château and the 11th-century fortress.

Near Ste Suzanne some enjoyable walks can be made in the Forêt de Grande Charnie, while just 7 km away is the bigger town of **Evron** (*52 km from Le Mans*), noted for its slaughter-houses but also for its splendid-looking basilica combining sturdy, simple Romanesque with graceful Gothic.

At the quiet riverside village of **Saulges** (*48 km from Le Mans*) there's an interesting parish church and, opposite, a remarkable little church dating right back to the 7th century. It's almost below ground level, and has traces of frescoes. Right next door is a good little two-star hotel-restaurant, **L'Ermitage** (tel. 43.90.52.28), with excellent and inexpensive menus.

LOIR VALLEY

From Vendôme to La Flèche: 100 km

Le Loir is La Loire on a much smaller, more human scale. Yet there are remarkable similarities between the grandest river in France and its little-known tributary. Along both, ornate Renaissance châteaux, mansions and whole villages are built of that spectacular stone, white tufa. There's good eating and good drinking to be done, too. The Loir is no vast, imposing valley, though; it's a picturesque river which can be closely followed on quiet country roads, with plenty of agreeable towns and villages perfect for a stroll, a café break or an overnight stop.

For a look at what the Loir valley has to offer, I have started my riverside journey in the Loir-et-Cher département, a few miles before it reaches the old boundaries of the county of Maine.

The modern industrial areas of **Vendôme** (*77 km from Le Mans*) are mainly well north of the river, and feel absolutely worlds away from the delightful old quarter. What really makes the place special is simply the river Loir, which breaks up into a multitude of confusing branches, creating the effect of a town built on four or five islands linked by a dozen bridges. Rising up on the south side is La Montagne, a steep hill crowned by the ruined 11th-century castle (altered in the 14th and 17th centuries) of the Counts of Vendôme. There's not much else to show the great age of the town, which was here before the Romans arrived. Various turbulent episodes – especially the Hundred Years War and the Religious Wars – led to wholesale destruction and subsequent rebuilding. The best survivor has been the abbey church of La Trinité. Its exuberant Flamboyant 16th-century façade aptly expresses the vision which caused Geoffroy Martel to found the abbey in 1040, of flaming swords descending from heaven. Apart from its elaborate front, this is a handsome buttressed building with many older sections, though none dates back to the original foundation. Detached from the rest stands a tall belfry from the 1150s.

Around the main square, Place St Martin, bars and brasseries invite a leisurely break over a coffee or aperitif. Or you could take it easy in the public gardens (the tourist office is here), right at the centre of the old quarter and almost enclosed by water. There are several good hotels and restaurants in this congenial town, though some are in the newer districts. **Hôtel Vendôme and Restaurant La Cloche Rouge** (15 Faubourg Chartrain, tel. 54.77.02.88) is well placed just across the right bank of the Loir, a few paces from the old quarter; it has a polite, impersonal air, modern, comfortable rooms and good menus all at moderate prices (much cheaper on weekdays, though, than at weekends).

Heading downriver on the country lanes, you pass through enjoyable and varied countryside, often with much worth halting to admire. Along the Loir (as on the Loire) there are often places where dwellings have been made in caves, or cut out of the riverside escarpments. Good examples can be seen at **Les Roques Évêques**, just before **Montoire-sur-le-Loir** (*70 km from Le Mans*). On the opposite side of the river, picturesque little **Lavardin** has a 12th-century church with fascinating wall paintings, as well as interesting ruins of an important 14th-century castle. There are some more intriguing cave houses, very impressive examples, at **Trôo**, 6 km further downstream. The village also preserves the remains of its ramparts and a notable 12th-century church – with another, even older, on the opposite bank at **St Jacques-des-Guérets**.

La Chartre-sur-le-Loir (*46 km from Le Mans*) is a contented country town with little to see, but with easy access to some lovely drives and walks as well as having a most satisfying and reliable two-star hotel-restaurant, **Hôtel de France**, in the main square (tel. 43.44.40.16).

Château du Loir (*40 km from Le Mans*) is larger and less interesting, with more traffic. Its name is confusing, too – there's no château (it was long ago dismantled, leaving hardly a trace), and it's not even on the Loir, but stands a couple of kilometres away on a tributary. Press on to **Le Lude** (*45 km from Le Mans*), a fine-looking old town with several Renaissance buildings and a grand château which deserves a visit, though it's only open in the afternoons from April to September. Interestingly, once a royal residence, it is today still lived in by a titled family. They contribute an atmosphere which helps you to remember that châteaux are not museums or monuments but essentially just houses. Ornate 18th-century chairs are, after all, simply chairs; the family have modern bits and pieces as well, while the dining-room wall is decorated with 16th-century Flemish tapestries. The château is a large edifice with a big circular tower at each corner, all arranged around a central courtyard. It covers many centuries in style, with a Gothic façade and Renaissance south wing, and stands in lovely grounds which run alongside the river Loir. It's the scene of spectacular *son et lumière* performances on summer weekend evenings; hundreds of local people take parts in an elaborate show with fireworks telling the history of the château and the town.

La Flèche (*42 km from Le Mans*) is another large town hectic with traffic, although it is redeemed by the river setting and a well-kept older quarter, mainly 17th century. The town hall on the bank of the Loir is most impressive: it's a former 17th-century château, with very agreeable public gardens. The one 'sight' is of more interest to the French than to the British: the Prytanée, an élite school for officers' sons, in a former Jesuit college. It was founded by Henri IV, who spent much of his childhood at La Flèche. One of the college's more famous

Bazouges Château

students was Descartes ('I think, therefore I am'). At **Bazouges**, 6 km downriver, pause on the narrow stone bridge for a view of this really attractive riverside village and its little château.

10. VAL DE LOIRE

parts of Loiret, Loir-et-Cher, Indre-et-Loire, Maine-et-Loire

Getting there

The Loire valley extends over a considerable distance from east to west, so the most suitable Channel port to use depends upon the final destination. Eastern stretches of the region (e.g. Orléans) are closest to Le Havre and Caen, and may even be best approached via Calais and Boulogne. The middle part of the valley (e.g. Tours) is within easy reach of Le Havre, Caen and St Malo. The western stretch (e.g. Angers) is closest to Caen and St Malo, with Cherbourg a little further away. The choice of port may also depend upon the arrival time of overnight crossings.

St Malo is 9 hours by day, 10¼ hours by night, from Portsmouth on Brittany Ferries, March to December. From June to September there are day and night crossings. In other months, night crossings only are operated, arriving at 8.15 a.m.

The Caen ferry port is at Ouistreham, 14 km from the city. Ouistreham is 6 hours from Portsmouth on Brittany Ferries. There are usually two daytime crossings and one at night (fewer in winter). Overnight crossings arrive at 6.30 a.m.

Cherbourg is 6 hours from Southampton (8 hours at night) on Sealink; 4¼ hours from Poole on Brittany Ferries' summer-only Truckline (5¼ hours at night); or 4¾ hours from Portsmouth on P&O (7½ hours at night). Sealink overnight ferries arrive at 9 a.m., P&O at 7 a.m., Truckline at 6 a.m. There are usually about two crossings daily from Portsmouth, three or four from Poole and one or two per day from Southampton.

Le Havre is 5¾ hours from Portsmouth (7 hours at night) on P&O, with usually three crossings daily. The overnight crossing arrives at 7 a.m.

TOWNS and villages along the Loire are certainly not too far away for a long weekend. An overnight crossing, an early arrival in France and a leisurely drive will bring you to the great valley by afternoon. Western parts, say downriver from Tours, are easier to reach than the more easterly towns. In high summer, the region is almost too popular for comfort, while conversely many fine châteaux are not open out of season. In addition, the climate is rather humid, warm and sultry on summer days, but unpleasantly chill and overcast in winter. Clearly, spring and autumn make the best times to spend a few days by the Loire.

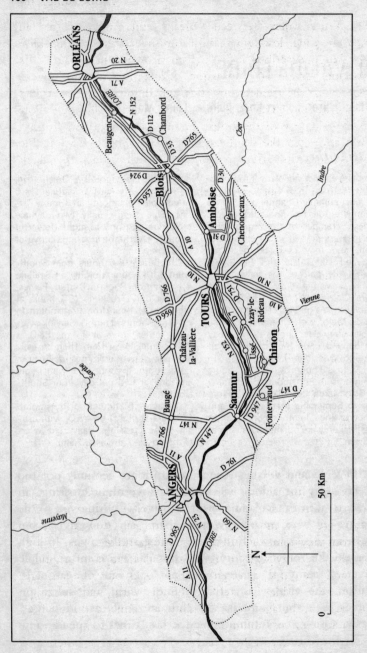

VAL DE LOIRE

The Loire valley between Orléans and Angers forms an immensely wide, low-lying landscape under vast, bright skies. Victor Hugo described it as 'a plain drowned in verdure'. Its proportions create an impression of magnificence entirely in keeping with the tremendous style and dignity long associated with the region. This stretch is the grandest in the whole changeable course of the Loire, France's longest river. From a modest spring in the southern hills of the Massif Central, the Loire gathers its strength running north along the flank of Burgundy; then, sweeping westwards on the approach to Orléans, it at last becomes, as the French call it, La Vallée des Rois, the Valley of Kings.

Here the valley expands to become the great Val de Loire of ornate Renaissance châteaux and delicate wines. Oddly enough, the river itself is almost the least of its charms, often lost from view behind reeds, trees and floodbanks. Rather, it is the human life of the valley – its civilization, food and wine, noble castles and old riverside towns and villages – which gives most pleasure.

The châteaux of the Loire, for the most part, are built of the white stone called tufa. This has the peculiar quality that, with passing decades, it becomes ever whiter and more beautiful, dazzling under jet-black slate roofs. Fairy-tale exteriors, fantastically decorative and conceived on a lavish scale, give the châteaux their distinctive character, reflecting the wealth and luxurious lifestyle of their former occupants. At the Revolution, when many of the owners of these ostentatious homes literally lost their heads, considerable damage was done, and, of course, valuables and furnishings were destroyed or removed. For that reason, it must be said, interiors may prove less pleasing. The châteaux are often most rewarding when seen from the outside only, from viewpoints within their private parklands.

Usually, the only way to visit a great château is on a guided tour – and the guide, as often as not, speaks only French. The main interest inside is likely to be historical, concentrating particularly on the age of the building, its family and their fate. Another tip: for maximum enjoyment of both the interior and the exterior of better-known châteaux, try to stay at a hotel close by and visit early in the morning – in that way, you can sometimes have the place almost to yourself.

Most Loire châteaux started life as medieval fortresses, but were reconstructed in the 16th and 17th centuries when questions of security could be replaced by a preoccupation with comfort and grace. Huge sums were spent on them. Many of the finest châteaux – as well as much of the prettiest countryside – are not on the Loire at all but along its beautiful tributaries: the Cher, the Indre and the Vienne.

For those who would rather tour than stay put, it's enjoyable to follow the course of the Loire either on minor roads (on the south side) or on busier routes nationales (on the north). Generally, the south or left bank is the more attractive, but bear in mind that the Loire is not always especially picturesque; some sections have plenty of industry, and the river has even been jokingly dubbed the *fleuve nucléaire* because of the number of nuclear power stations along its length. Yet everywhere the valley and river possess a unique grandeur.

The whole region – towns, cities and villages – is liberally sprinkled with first-class restaurants. Michelin rosettes abound. So too do excellent traditional hotels; indeed, some of the châteaux, still (despite the Revolution) owned and occupied by aristocratic families, nowadays take paying guests – it's hard to imagine a more fitting way than that to experience the valley of the Loire.

À table

The Val de Loire region was not historically important for its gastronomy, although certainly there is good fish and excellent fruit and vegetables. However, the long-term influence of the many aristocratic homes along the Loire and its tributaries has been a concern with quality, taste and good living. Nowadays the Loire valley can be considered one of the country's leading gastronomic regions – with styles of cooking, and chefs, imported from all over France.

Yet the Loire does have favourite dishes of its own. Fish stews, often with eels, are frequently served. There's plenty of charcuterie, much of it incorporating game. Salads are dressed with local walnut oil and red wine vinegar. Small, nutty goats' cheeses and mild, creamy white cows' milk cheeses are found in the local markets. The Touraine area, the heart of the region, is noted for prunes, which are added to savoury dishes. For dessert, pastries containing plenty of fruit are popular – *tarte tatin*, the delicious upside-down cake filled with caramelized eating apples, originated from Lamotte-Beuvron, just south of Orléans. You will often find it on local menus.

Where the Loire may lay a greater claim is for its wines, with numerous excellent *appellations*. Despite a considerable diversity in styles, from light reds and rosés to whites which can be anything from crisply dry to sweet and sparkling, there is nevertheless such a thing as a Loire character in wine: agreeable fruity flavour and a light freshness. Some of the best Loire wines do not come from within our 'weekend' region, but they will still prove readily available, and are considered local. For example, Pouilly-sur-Loire and Sancerre, two towns facing each other across the water a few miles upriver, both produce exquisite dry whites. Other leading wine towns and villages are Vouvray (first-class whites of every type), Chinon (fruity reds and some whites) and Saumur (superb sparkling whites and reds). At the cheaper end of the scale is the ubiquitous crisp, tasty and refreshing white wine called Sauvignon de Touraine.

ORLÉANS

280 km from Caen/Ouistreham, 284 km from Le Havre

At the centre of the extensive area of modern Orléans is the ancient waterside heart of the city. This historic quarter, with old streets and houses, cathedral and museums, extends along the north bank. Impressive but rather austere in appearance, it is best admired from the other side of the river.

Not surprisingly the town makes much of its patriotic and devout heroine Joan of Arc, alias the Maid of Orléans. However, the soubriquet does not mean she was an Orléans girl;

Joan came from the Vosges in north-east France. In May 1429 she rode, armour-clad and triumphant, despite a fresh arrow wound sustained in the battle, into the city from which she had driven the English troops. Place du Martroi, the focus of the old quarter, is dominated by a statue of Joan on horseback with sword raised to heaven. The main street to the huge, wonderfully elaborate Gothic cathedral of Ste Croix is called after her, too, and in the cathedral she is celebrated in stained glass. In Place Général de Gaulle, the Centre Jeanne d'Arc, in the house (rebuilt) where Joan supposedly stayed in 1429, tells the story of her life and victory.

Next door to the cathedral, there's something which, at last, is nothing to do with Joan, the town's excellent Fine Arts Museum. It displays a full range of French painting from the 15th century onwards, including a few good Impressionist and Post-Impressionist works by Boudin, Courbet, Max Jacob and Gauguin. Adjacent to the museum, the city's town hall is a distinctive redbrick Renaissance mansion called Hôtel Groslot. Caryatids flank the entrance. Built in 1530, it was reworked in the 19th century, but in its earlier form was a noble enough residence for several kings to stay here while in Orléans. There are several other elegant mansions around the old centre, some of them now housing museums.

There's some good shopping to be done in Orléans, especially for high-quality foods. You will discover wonderful chocolatiers, pâtissiers, fromageries and charcutiers in Rue de Bourgogne (which was the main street of the original Gallo-Roman city on this site), as well as in the covered market off Rue Royale, and in the handsomely arcaded Rue Royale itself, a busy street ideal for a spree of buying anything and everything.

Rue Royale runs from Place Martroi to Pont George V. Cross the river on this attractive 18th-century bridge, which was called Pont Royal until renamed in 1920 to show that the city bore no ill will to the English despite the Hundred Years War! On the south side of the river Olivet is an attractive area of market gardens and flower nurseries. Close by, the Parc Floral de la Source is a lovely 74-acre park of gorgeous flower-beds, splashing fountains and stately old trees. The source in question is that of the Loiret, a Loire tributary which reappears here having disappeared underground near its true source several miles away at St Benoît-sur-Loire.

Orléans has many hotels old and new, and several excellent restaurants. Two deserve special mention: **Les Antiquaires** (2–4 Rue au Lin, tel. 38.53.52.35), with first-class game dishes, perfect service and superb wines; and **La Crémaillère** (34 Rue Notre-Dame de Recouvrance, tel. 38.53.49.17), where a Breton chef shows how a simple approach to fine ingredients can produce brilliant results. Prices at both are above average, but not excessive.

BEAUGENCY

21 km from Orléans

The cobbled streets of Beaugency retain a good deal of medieval atmosphere, and the splendid 14th-century stone bridge with its twenty-two irregular arches spans the Loire as grandly as ever. Locals tell the unlikely tale that it was the Devil himself who built this fine construction, in exchange for the soul of the first Beaugency inhabitant to cross it. Fortunately, the first was only a cat. Or perhaps not so fortunately, for it turns out that all Beaugency residents are nicknamed *chats*.

In summer the little town becomes rather overcrowded with tourists. They come to see the picturesque old quarter around Place St Firmin, the ruins of the 11th-century castle keep and the agreeable riverside walk. Come slightly out of season to enjoy it in tranquillity. There are two hotels, both in historic buildings full of character, that I particularly like here: the large **Hôtel de l'Abbaye** (Quai Abbaye, tel. 38.44.67.35), occupying part of Beaugency's austere 17th-century abbey, with a lovely waterside garden; and **L'Écu de Bretagne** (Place du Martroi, tel. 38.44.67.60), a warmer, homelier, creakier old inn overlooking a square in the centre of the little town. Both have first-rate restaurants.

BLOIS AND AROUND

56 km from Orléans, 58 km from Tours

Ancient Blois, a small town constructed largely of white stone roofed with distinctive blue slate, rises on the north bank of the Loire. Its picturesque lanes are watched over by an immense château, a jumble of styles and additions, a favourite of the French monarchy for generations. Interior decorations are lavish and skilful although furnishing is disappointingly lacking, except in the apartments of Catherine de Medici. The building's wonderful exterior spiral staircase is a masterpiece of Renaissance art and craftsmanship. The Château de Blois earned a notorious place in French history with the savage murder of the Duke de Guise actually inside the apartment of the King, Henri III, who felt that the Duke posed a threat to him. Clearly, in those days they went in for a more literal type of political back-stabbing than we do now! East of the château there's an especially picturesque older quarter. The main shopping street, Rue Denis Papin, has some tempting food specialists. Seen from the south side of the river, Blois looks particularly attractive.

Head south-east from the town to one of the most spectacular and impressive of all the Loire valley châteaux: **Chambord**. In the midst of a vast forest, it was once no more than a fortified hunting lodge. King François I, who had a passion for hunting, transformed the building into the most regal of country retreats. Fittingly it is the roof which crowns the affair, a mass of spires, turrets, windows and ornamentation rising above the treetops. Inside are impressive halls, a grand staircase and over 400 rooms, everything loaded with Renaissance decoration. It is satisfying to stand on the terraces from which royalty once watched the forest hunt, and realize that now the huge woodland is a preserve in which the animals – including wild boar – are protected.

AMBOISE AND AROUND

24 km from Tours

An agreeable, compact old town on the south bank of the Loire, Amboise amply rewards a short visit. It was here that Leonardo da Vinci, staying as a guest of the King, François I, became fascinated by the soft brightness of the light over the wide Loire valley. His great longing, he said, was to be able to 'render this light accurately' on canvas. The last three years of his life were spent living in the town at Le Manoir du Clos Lucé, now an intriguing museum of Leonardo's scientific designs and plans. The château of Amboise, poised on terraces high above the town and river, looks its best from across the water on the north bank. Both Louis XI and Charles VII were born here. It's a patched-up building which has suffered much in various wars, but remains the dominant presence in the town. Below the castle there's an attractive – though often crowded – cluster of pedestrianized medieval streets.

Fifteen kilometres upriver, road and river pass together beneath the lofty château of **Chaumont** in its clifftop gardens. Catherine de Medici, who stayed as a guest in most of the region's best châteaux, owned Chaumont until, by a certain amount of double-dealing, she managed to swap it for its much grander neighbour, the château of **Chenonceau**, a short distance south.

Chenonceau has become possibly the most popular of all the Loire châteaux. The coach parties and endless stream of visitors arriving by car inevitably detract from the dignity of the place, yet it is still admirable. This truly is an exquisite flight of imagination, as well as an astonishing achievement in construction. It was Diane de Poitiers's idea – she was Chenonceau's owner before Catherine – to build a wing on to the palace which, standing on pillars in the water, would go clear across the adjacent river Cher. The result was a brilliant success. Elegant gardens in the formal French style, looking like a huge carpet laid on the ground, and a sumptuous interior, complete the effect. During part of the Second World War the château

Château at Chenonceaux

provided a curious escape route from the German-occupied zone on the east bank to the free area on the west. Note that while the castle is spelt Chenonceau, the neighbouring village (now turned over almost entirely to catering for visitors) is spelt Chenonceaux.

Bléré (*23 km from Tours*), just 7 km down the Cher from Chenonceaux, is a delightfully unpretentious workaday small town. It might otherwise be hard to recommend a detour to Bléré, since it really cannot boast anything of note – except for a little hotel-restaurant which is one of my favourites: **Le Cheval Blanc** (Place de l'Église, tel. 47.30.30.14), run by the likeable Michel and Micheline Blériot. Michel is a superb chef, and makes good use of the fresh produce of local small farmers as well as having his own large and productive vegetable and herb garden. His standards are high and prices moderate.

Travelling downriver from Amboise, stay on the north bank to pass through **Vouvray** (*10 km from Tours*), home of several of the Loire's most prestigious wines, before entering Tours. Or travel along the south side of the river to see many strange cave-houses carved into the tufa cliffs.

TOURS

244 km from Caen/Ouistreham

Tours is at the heart of châteaux country. The city stands on a curious peninsula, a long sliver of land between the Loire and the Cher. It's a place of some style, with chic shopping and more than a dozen excellent restaurants. Indeed, to the French mind, Tours is the very essence of what the aristocratic châteaux are all about. It has a reputation for civilization, refinement and *savoir-vivre*; the Tours accent is considered the 'best' in France.

Yet it offers surprisingly little to see. Its château has been demolished, and much of the old town was damaged in the last war. Nevertheless what remains of the historic district down by the river is attractive and full of interest. Rue Nationale, the modern main shopping street, runs straight down from the central Place Jean-Jaurès to the banks of the Loire. To either side are older streets of character: to the left, Vieux Tours, the historic centre; and to the right, the even more ancient cathedral quarter. Beside the crumbling Flamboyant Gothic grandeur of the cathedral, and next to a remnant of the town's original Gallo-Roman ramparts, the former Episcopal Palace stands shaded by a glorious cedar of Lebanon almost two centuries old. Today the building houses an extensive Fine Arts Musuem. On the other side of the cathedral is the surviving fragment of Henry Plantagenet's château beside a lovely riverside walkway.

Stroll along here to the end of Rue Nationale, where statues of Descartes and Rabelais contemplate the capricious flow of the Loire and, no doubt, of life. Behind them, inside the chapter house and monks' dormitory of St Julien's church, are the Musée du Compagnonnage (Museum of Trade Guilds) and a museum of local wines, both worth a visit. Vieux Tours has been skilfully restored, its narrow streets closed to traffic, and has become the most picturesque part of town. This is a good district, too, to find enjoyable bars and restaurants. However, the best of Touraine gastronomy is found on the Loire's right bank. In particular, **Jean Bardet's** hotel-restaurant (57 Rue

Groison, tel. 47.41.41.11) is a leading light of French cuisine and a haven of peace and civilization – pricey, though.

CHINON AND AROUND

45 km from Tours

The delightful and atmospheric old town of Chinon rises from the north bank of the river Vienne. Rabelais, inspired by the palatable local red wine, lived here and gathered his colourful characters and sometimes rather bawdy stories. There's plenty of interest to be discovered. The ancient (6th–12th-century) chapel of St Radegonde can be found inside a cave, and there are several other remarkable medieval churches, as well as a good Museum of Old Chinon. There are fine mansions, and several streets, notably Rue Voltaire and Grand Carroi, full of handsome 14th- and 15th-century timbered dwellings.

On a lofty ridge at the western end of town stands the impressive shell of a once great château. It's a complicated building in several sections, but one can only try to imagine just how impressive and well defended it must have been. Cardinal Richelieu purchased the mighty fortress in the 17th century, and through a combination of neglect and active dismantling (Richelieu used the stone to build another mansion for himself) it was virtually destroyed. In earlier centuries, though, this castle had been of tremendous importance, a dwelling certainly fit for kings. Henry II, the Plantagenet King of England who married Eleanor of Aquitaine and gained half of western France in her dowry, died here in 1189. And in 1429 after the kingdom of France had already been signed away to the English, in the Great Hall of the château's royal apartments a girl called Jehan la Pucelle – Joan the Maid – picked out the future Charles VII from a crowd of his courtiers and announced that she had been told by God that he must go to Reims to be crowned King of France. Joan then led the victorious battle which turned the tide against the English and caused her prophecy to be fulfilled.

Chinon has had its shameful moments too, as when, in 1321,

Ussé

the people of the town gathered the local Jews together – 160
men, women and children – and burned them alive on the island
which lies in mid-river at this point.

There's an outstanding restaurant at Chinon, **Au Plaisir
Gourmand** (Quai Charles VII, tel. 47.93.20.48), in a charming
house in the fascinating little district between the château and
the river. The food is marvellous, but it's not cheap, and you'll
need to book well ahead. There's also a popular old hotel in
town, the **Hostellerie Gargantua** (73 Rue Haute St Maurice,
tel. 47.93.04.71), noted for character, moderate prices and good
hearty cooking.

Oak forests stretch from here to the château at **Azay-le-
Rideau** (*20 km from Chinon, 27 km from Tours*). This was the
first of the Loire's medieval fortresses to be converted into a

Fontevraud-abbey entrance

Renaissance palace, and one can perhaps tell that the change was made under a woman's hand, that of the wife of financier Philippe Lesbahy. Enclosed by woods and reflected in its lake, little Azay set a standard of delicacy, elegance and style which few others were ever to match. Its earlier fortifications have been delightfully imitated with ornamental turrets. The pretty river Indre provides a moat. Azay village, although often crowded, is also very appealing, and has several friendly small hotels and restaurants offering a good standard at a reasonable price.

Where the Chinon forest touches the Loire, where the river Indre also flows alongside, the gleaming white château at **Ussé** (*15 km from Chinon, 50 km from Tours*) looks like something out of a children's picture-book, and so it should: it was the setting for the story Sleeping Beauty. It is still an aristocrat's home, and can be visited on guided tours.

On the border between the Touraine and Anjou, **Fontevraud l'Abbaye** (*20 km from Chinon, 53 km from Tours*) is a hilltop village, all in lovely pale stone, with a beautiful historic abbey at its heart. The old abbey is now a modern 'cultural centre', where concerts, art exhibitions and *son et lumières* are held during the balmy summer months. Fontevraud was where many a person of noble birth decided to seek refuge from the world. It was unusual in that both men and women were accepted, under the rule of an abbess. It is hard to believe that this glorious place was a prison from Napoleonic times until 1972. The parish church outside the abbey limits has an unusual and attractive exterior, while all around the little town the Forêt de Fontevraud provides pleasing country for walks.

Anjou is noted not just for castles but for wine. **Montsoreau**, on the Loire's south bank (*20 km from Chinon, 53 km from Tours*), has both. So does charming old **Saumur** (*30 km from Chinon, 64 km from Tours*), which rises from the banks of the Loire and is the centre of a district specializing in excellent *méthode champenoise* sparkling white wine. Saumur's huge sturdy castle, surrounded by the town's old quarter, stands high with a commanding view. The Saumur wine-makers are mostly based out of town at **St Hilaire-St Florent**.

ANGERS

200 km from St Malo, 224 km from Caen

Anjou's capital strikes a very different note from the rest of the château country. For a start, it is noisy, busy and intent upon earning its living. It does not stand on the Loire but 8 km away on the river Maine. And there's little sign of the lovely white tufa so much used in the other great cities of the Val de Loire region. Here the buildings are made instead of dark stone, although there is 'light relief' in the paler-coloured surrounding modern districts. For that reason, together with the fact that the town is a prosperous commercial and manufacturing centre with little need to encourage tourism, Angers attracts relatively few visitors.

None the less there is plenty of interest in this imposing old city. The superb riverside château, once home of 'Good King Réné' of Anjou and Provence, has seventeen great towers striped with layers of light and dark stone. The towers look daunting enough today, but were once even more awesome, before

Henry III ordered the castle to be demolished. The work was begun, but got no further than reducing the towers to the level of the curtain wall, by which time Henry had died. The château terrace gives a good view over the river. Cross a drawbridge to enter the fortress. Inside, there's a marvellous collection of tapestries dating from the 14th to 17th centuries. The most outstanding is the huge six-centuries-old Apocalypse Tapestry of 1380, which depicts the vision of St John. Incredibly, this wonderful piece of work was thrown into the streets by Revolutionaries and cut to shreds by the local people. It was fifty years later that efforts were made to recover the fragments, and, equally incredibly, most of the tapestry was recovered and expertly repaired.

Angers has a reputation as a centre of art and culture. The Musée Jean Lurçat, on the other side of the river, houses modern tapestries, including Lurçat's latter-day version of the Apocalypse, with a poignantly different conclusion from the original. Back on the south bank of the Maine, the 15th-century Renaissance mansion Logis Barrault is home to an important Musée des Beaux-Arts (Fine Arts Museum) with 18th- and 19th-century painting, sculpture and furnishings. More sculpture, all by David of Angers, is displayed in a gallery inside a 13th-century former abbey in Rue Toussant. It's worth paying a visit to the 12th-century cathedral, further along Rue Toussant, to see its excellent stained glass. A long, shallow flight of steps, on which local students often lounge, descends gracefully from the cathedral to the river. A more beautiful church is St Serge, along Rue Boreau. It has a wonderful 12th-century choir, and stained glass of the 16th century.

The main square, Place du Ralliement, is full of life and offers a choice of popular bars and brasseries. The surrounding streets have some interesting old houses, as well as a number of excellent restaurants.

For somewhere to stay, I would recommend finding a village out of town – Angers is best seen on a day visit from some quieter base. One possibility is **Chalonnes-sur-Loire** (*22 km from Angers*), an attractive small town on the bank of the broad island-studded river Loire towards Nantes. It has a cobbled quayside, an appealing atmosphere and a decent, inexpensive hotel, the **Hôtel de France** (5 Rue Nationale, tel. 41.78.00.12).

INDEX

Hotels and restaurants with names beginning with Le, Les, etc., are indexed under the word following. Page locations in **bold type** denote main references.

FOR THE BEST IN PAPERBACKS, LOOK FOR THE

In every corner of the world, on every subject under the sun, Penguin represents quality and variety – the very best in publishing today.

For complete information about books available from Penguin – including Puffins, Penguin Classics and Arkana – and how to order them, write to us at the appropriate address below. Please note that for copyright reasons the selection of books varies from country to country.

In the United Kingdom: Please write to *Dept E.P., Penguin Books Ltd, Harmondsworth, Middlesex, UB7 0DA.*

If you have any difficulty in obtaining a title, please send your order with the correct money, plus ten per cent for postage and packaging, to *PO Box No 11, West Drayton, Middlesex*

In the United States: Please write to *Dept BA, Penguin, 299 Murray Hill Parkway, East Rutherford, New Jersey 07073*

In Canada: Please write to *Penguin Books Canada Ltd, 2801 John Street, Markham, Ontario L3R 1B4*

In Australia: Please write to the *Marketing Department, Penguin Books Australia Ltd, P.O. Box 257, Ringwood, Victoria 3134*

In New Zealand: Please write to the *Marketing Department, Penguin Books (NZ) Ltd, Private Bag, Takapuna, Auckland 9*

In India: Please write to *Penguin Overseas Ltd, 706 Eros Apartments, 56 Nehru Place, New Delhi, 110019*

In the Netherlands: Please write to *Penguin Books Netherlands B.V., Postbus 3507, 1001 AH, Amsterdam*

In West Germany: Please write to *Penguin Books Ltd, Friedrichstrasse 10–12, D–6000 Frankfurt/Main 1*

In Spain: Please write to *Alhambra Longman S.A., Fernandez de la Hoz 9, E–28010 Madrid*

In Italy: Please write to *Penguin Italia s.r.l., Via Como 4, I-20096 Pioltello (Milano)*

In France: Please write to *Penguin Books Ltd, 39 Rue de Montmorency, F-75003 Paris*

In Japan: Please write to *Longman Penguin Japan Co Ltd, Yamaguchi Building, 2–12–9 Kanda Jimbocho, Chiyoda-Ku, Tokyo 101*

A CHOICE OF PENGUINS

Riding the Iron Rooster Paul Theroux

An eye-opening and entertaining account of travels in old and new China, from the author of *The Great Railway Bazaar*. 'Mr Theroux cannot write badly ... in the course of a year there was almost no train in the vast Chinese rail network on which he did not travel' – Ludovic Kennedy

The Life of Graham Greene Norman Sherry
Volume One 1904–1939

'Probably the best biography ever of a living author' – Philip French in the *Listener*. Graham Greene has always maintained a discreet distance from his reading public. This volume reconstructs his first thirty-five years to create one of the most revealing literary biographies of the decade.

The Chinese David Bonavia

'I can think of no other work which so urbanely and entertainingly succeeds in introducing the general Western reader to China' – *Sunday Telegraph*

All the Wrong Places James Fenton

Who else but James Fenton could have played a Bach prelude on the presidential piano – and stolen one of Imelda's towels – on the very day Marcos left his palace in Manila? 'He is the most professional of amateur war correspondents, a true though unusual journo, top of the trade. When he arrives in town, prudent dictators pack their bags and quit' – *The Times*

Voices of the Old Sea Norman Lewis

'Limpidly and lovingly, Norman Lewis has caught the helpless, unwitting, often foolish, but always hopeful village in its dying summers, and saved the tragedy with sublime comedy' – *Observer*

Ninety-Two Days Evelyn Waugh

With characteristic honesty, Evelyn Waugh here debunks the romantic notions attached to rough travelling. His journey in Guiana and Brazil is difficult, dangerous and extremely uncomfortable, and his account of it is witty and unquestionably compelling.

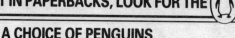
A CHOICE OF PENGUINS

The Assassination of Federico García Lorca   Ian Gibson

Lorca's 'crime' was his antipathy to pomposity, conformity and intolerance. His punishment was murder. Ian Gibson – author of the acclaimed new biography of Lorca – reveals the truth about his death and the atmosphere in Spain that allowed it to happen.

Between the Woods and the Water   Patrick Leigh Fermor

Patrick Leigh Fermor continues his celebrated account – begun in *A Time of Gifts* – of his journey on foot from the Hook of Holland to Constantinople. 'Even better than everyone says it is' – Peter Levi. 'Indescribably rich and beautiful' – *Guardian*

The Time Out Film Guide   Edited by Tom Milne

The definitive, up-to-the-minute directory of 9,000 films – world cinema from classics and silent epics to reissues and the latest releases – assessed by two decades of *Time Out* reviewers. 'In my opinion the best and most comprehensive' – Barry Norman

Metamagical Themas   Douglas R. Hofstadter

This astonishing sequel to the bestselling, Pulitzer Prize-winning *Gödel, Escher, Bach* swarms with 'extraordinary ideas, brilliant fables, deep philosophical questions and Carrollian word play' – Martin Gardner

Into the Heart of Borneo   Redmond O'Hanlon

'Perceptive, hilarious and at the same time a serious natural-history journey into one of the last remaining unspoilt paradises' – *New Statesman*. 'Consistently exciting, often funny and erudite without ever being overwhelming' – *Punch*

When the Wind Blows   Raymond Briggs

'A visual parable against nuclear war: all the more chilling for being in the form of a strip cartoon' – *Sunday Times*. 'The most eloquent anti-Bomb statement you are likely to read' – *Daily Mail*